W9-CHI-379

Reading the Future: A Portrait of Literacy in Canada

Published by authority of the Minister responsible for Statistics Canada

September 1996

Price: Canada: $49.00

United States: US$59.00

Other countries: US$69.00

Catalogue no. 89-551-XPE

Frequency: Occasional

ISBN 0-660-16514-7

Ottawa

Statistics Canada
Human Resources Development Canada
National Literacy Secretariat

Canadian Cataloguing in Publication Data

Main entry under title:

Reading the future : a portrait of literacy
in Canada

Co-published by: Human Resources Development
Canada, National Literacy Secretariat.
Published also in French under title: Lire
l'avenir : un portrait de l'alphabétisme au
Canada.
ISBN 0-660-16514-7
CS89-551-XPE

1. Literacy Canada — Canada. 2. Literacy —
Canada — Statistics. 3. Functional literacy —
Canada. I. Statistics Canada. II. Canada.
National Literacy Secretariat.

LC514 R42 1996   374'.012'0971
C96-988015-4

Foreword

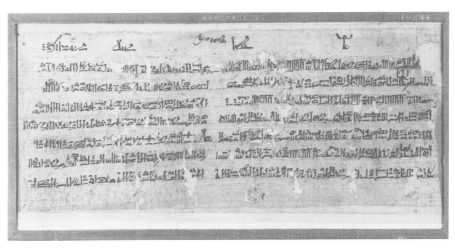

Part of a papyrus written by a student scribe, containing corrections added at the top by his master. The words in the text to which the corrections refer are underlined. The errors include misspellings and poor hieratic signs. Above the space between the columns of text, a date is written: 3rd month of summer, day 23'; it probably indicates the day on which the texts were written.

The contents of papyri written by student scribes usually consist of short passages concerned with everyday matters, descriptive pieces with difficult words, formal letters and moral instructions. Here, the right-hand column contains a letter of congratulation to an army officer, the left-hand column a letter dealing with matters relating to a bull.

Nineteenth Dynasty, c. 1210 B.C. Thebes

© Reproduced with permission from the British Museum.

This report contains startling insights into the central role literacy plays in determining individual economic success in Canada. It is important, however, to keep this fact and the concerns the report raises about the future of the national economy and social development in proper perspective. As illustrated by the foregoing caption, literacy has helped to shape economies and societies for thousands of years. What makes literacy so important in the current context is its potential to make societies more cohesive and give a country an economic advantage in the global markets of the information age.

T. Scott Murray
International Study Director for the International Adult Literacy Survey,
Statistics Canada

Note of appreciation

Canada owes the success of its statistical system to the long-standing co-operation of Statistics Canada, the citizens of Canada, its businesses, governments and other institutions. Accurate and timely statistical information could not be produced without their continued co-operation and goodwill.

Contents

List of tables

List of figures

Introduction

The International Adult Literacy Survey (IALS) was a seven-country initiative conducted in the fall of 1994. Its goal: to create comparable literacy profiles across national, linguistic and cultural boundaries. The results demonstrated a strong plausible link between literacy and a country's economic potential.

The International Adult Literacy Survey (IALS) was a seven-country initiative conducted in the fall of 1994. Its goal: to create comparable literacy profiles across national, linguistic and cultural boundaries. The results, published in the report *Literacy, Economy and Society: Results of the first International Adult Literacy Survey* (Organisation for Economic Co-operation and Development and Statistics Canada 1995), demonstrated a strong plausible link between literacy and a country's economic potential.

This Canadian report expands and extends the analysis of the Canadian data presented in the international report, including additional data on the distribution of literacy by region and language.

The Canadian component of the IALS study was primarily funded by the Applied Research Branch and the National Literacy Secretariat of Human Resources Development Canada. Additional funding was also provided by the governments of New Brunswick, Ontario and Alberta. Finally, the sample of respondents over 65 years of age was augmented with the financial support of the Seniors Secretariat of Health Canada.

Skills and human capital

With today's unprecedented levels of global competitiveness, countries are quickly beginning to see the need to develop and nurture their own human capital. The individual is, more than ever, a central component in a nation's economic success. The development of basic skills and lifelong learning are being promoted by many countries, in hopes of improving their economic health and the human condition of their citizens. Literacy is central to such goals. Without the ability to read and process information, further learning becomes both time consuming and expensive for participants, a fact that limits their economic success and life chances. Clearly, countries with an adequately trained work force have the short-term edge; however, those with a flexible work force will be best able to adapt to economic and social challenges.

Just as global societies are redefining themselves, the concept of literacy is undergoing an evolution of its own. Theoretical and technological advances have transformed literacy from a simple dichotomy into a richer, more complex construct. More important than the simple ability to read, literacy now focuses on the ability to *use* information from printed texts. This focus places the practice of literacy in a realistic context. Moreover, the new framework defines a structured continuum of abilities that recognizes various degrees of literacy skill along a well-defined range of reading materials.

Goals and structure

The IALS was designed to meet seven objectives:[1]

- to provide comparative data on adults and workers in countries that constitute a cross-section of Canada's current and emerging trading partners;[2]

- to provide an updated profile of adult literacy skills for Canada for comparison with that provided by the 1989 Survey of Literacy Skills Used in Daily Activities (LSUDA);[3]

- to provide better data on several special subpopulations of particular national policy interest;

- to shed light on the relationship between performance, educational attainment, labour market participation and employment for those individuals found to be able to read but not able to do so very well;

- to test the notion that the decoding and decision-making skills embodied in the Canadian and United States assessments are stable across language groups and cultures;

- to promote the concept of literacy underlying the direct assessments conducted in Canada and the United States; and

- to compare and contrast the literacy skill profiles for economically important subpopulations across countries and language groups.

The results of the Survey of Literacy Skills Used in Daily Activities (LSUDA), a survey of over 9,000 adults aged 16 to 69 conducted by Statistics Canada in 1989, revealed a wide range of literacy skills in Canada's adult population.[4] A series of studies based on the LSUDA data enriched the understanding of adult literacy in the nation.[5] These studies also identified new questions that were important to understanding adult reading skill.[6] The 1994 International Adult Literacy Survey (IALS) was designed to address several of these questions.

The need to generate comparative data for several countries required the basic LSUDA study design to be modified in several respects. For example, IALS chose to adopt both the literacy domains and the literacy proficiency levels developed for the United States National Adult Literacy Survey (NALS). Thus, the IALS provides data for three distinct literacy domains:

- *Prose literacy*—the knowledge and skills needed to understand and use information from texts including editorials, news stories, poems and fiction;

- *Document literacy*—the knowledge and skills required to locate and use information contained in various formats, including job applications, payroll forms, transportation schedules, maps, tables and graphics; and

---

1. For a complete description of the IALS goals, see *An International Assessment of Adult Literacy: A Proposal*, Statistics Canada 1992.

2. The goal in conducting the cross-country comparisons was not to rank the participating countries, but to see whether the relationships found in Canada between literacy and other characteristics were also found in other countries. A compendium of the international comparative data has been published (*Literacy, Economy and Society: Results of the first International Adult Literacy Survey*, Organisation for Economic Co-operation and Development and Statistics Canada 1995) and the full set of data is not repeated here.

3. *Adult Literacy in Canada: Results of a National Study*, Statistics Canada 1991.

4. See footnote 3.

5. *Reading, but not reading well: Reading skills at Level 3*, Stan Jones 1993; *Adult Literacy in America: A First Look at the Results of the National Adult Literacy Survey*, Kirsch et al. 1993.

6. See, for example, "Toward an explanatory model of document literacy," *Discourse Processes*, Peter B. Mosenthal and Irwin S. Kirsch 1991.

● *Quantitative literacy*—the knowledge and skills required to apply arithmetic operations, either alone or sequentially, to numbers embedded in printed materials, such as balancing a chequebook, figuring out a tip, completing an order form or determining the amount of interest on a loan from an advertisement.[7]

These changes also reflect our improved understanding of literacy as a cognitive activity, an understanding derived from analysis of the LSUDA survey and a series of national studies conducted in the United States.[8]

To achieve the third objective, some groups were oversampled so that sufficient numbers would be available for analysis: Unemployment Insurance and social assistance recipients, in- and out-of-school youth, and francophones in New Brunswick and Ontario. The IALS also provided an opportunity to collect data on the literacy skills of older Canadians. The LSUDA survey did not include anyone over 69 in the sample. It was thought that the skills of those older than 69 were lower than the skills of those aged 65 to 69; therefore estimates could be made of the need for literacy education in the older population. However, it is better to have more direct measures. In addition, the LSUDA background questionnaire was extensively modified to explore some of the interesting relationships uncovered by the LSUDA and other literacy studies.

The goal of this Canadian report is to further explore and extend the analysis of the IALS dataset, paying close attention to issues of particular interest to Canadian public policy. The Introduction provides some key findings and presents the conceptual framework for understanding and interpreting literacy levels on the three scales used in the analysis. It complements Appendix B; together, they will help readers understand the survey results.

Chapters 1 through 3 of this report have been written primarily by Stan Jones, a researcher in adult education. Using the same structure as the international report, Chapter 1 presents a detailed description of the distribution of literacy, answering the questions, "What is literacy in Canada?" and "How is it distributed?" This chapter includes an examination of the links to the 1989 Survey of Literacy Skills Used in Daily Activities (LSUDA) study. It also presents a profile of literacy in Canada based on several demographic characteristics, including educational attainment, age, gender and language. Chapter 2 deals with the question of why literacy is important, by offering a link between literacy and the economic success of individuals and, by extension, our nation. Then, Chapter 3 discusses the practices of literacy in detail, showing how literacy is both attained and maintained in the workplace and at home. The concluding chapter examines the success of the IALS model in light of the trends and findings presented and highlights the importance of literacy to individual decisions and public policy. It also points to some avenues where the IALS data merit further investigation.

---

7. Quantitative literacy as defined in the IALS is roughly equivalent to the term "numeracy" used in Canada's 1989 Survey of Literacy Skills Used in Daily Activities.

8. *Literacy: Profiles of America's Young Adults*, Irwin S. Kirsch and Ann Jungeblut 1986; *Beyond the School Doors: The Literacy Needs of Job Seekers Served by the U.S. Department of Labor*, Kirsch et al. 1992; *Adult Literacy in America: A First Look at the Results of the National Adult Literacy Survey*, Kirsch et al. 1993.

Eight key findings

The key findings of this report can be summarized in eight points:[9]

- Important differences in literacy skills exist, both within and among countries. These differences are large enough to matter both socially and economically. The differences in skill observed in Canada across demographic groups are large.

- Literacy is strongly associated with economic life chances and opportunities. This affects employment stability, the incidence of unemployment, and income, among other things.

- In North America, scores on the quantitative literacy scale provide the strongest correlates to income. There is a large "income bonus" in Canada and the United States for literacy proficiency at the highest level (Level 4/5).

- Literacy skill levels are clearly linked to occupations and industries; some occupations need high level skills, and others reflect requirements for intermediate skills.

- Literacy's relationship to educational attainment is complex. While the association with education is strong, it also offers some surprising exceptions. For example, some adults have managed to attain a relatively high degree of literacy proficiency despite a low level of education. Conversely, there are some who have low literacy skills despite a high level of education. Objective skill testing is obviously emerging as a preferred tool to enable more rigorous evaluation of the real skills of the work force.

- Low literacy skill levels are found not just among marginalized groups, but also among large proportions of the entire adult population. The IALS data show that adult education and training programs are less likely to reach those with low skills, because most training goes to those with high skills.

- Adults with low literacy skills do not usually report that their skills present them with any difficulties. When asked if their reading skills were sufficient to meet their everyday needs, most respondents replied overwhelmingly that they were, regardless of tested skill levels. This may reflect the fact that many occupy jobs that do not require the use of literacy, a fact which is likely to change.

- Literacy skills, like muscles, are maintained and strengthened through regular use. While formal education provides a more or less required base, the evidence indicates that applying literacy skills in daily activities—both at home and at work—is associated with higher levels of performance.

Antecedents of the IALS

Building on the works of Irwin Kirsch at the Educational Testing Service in Princeton, New Jersey, and Peter Mosenthal of the Reading and Language Arts Center of Syracuse University in New York, several pioneering studies have been carried out that have successfully advanced the understanding of a conceptual

---

9. Derived in part from the conclusion (pp. 115–118) of the report *Literacy, Economy and Society: Results of the first International Adult Literacy Survey* (Organisation for Economic Co-operation and Development and Statistics Canada 1995), which gives more detail on these broad conclusions.

definition of literacy and its relationship to individual and national socio-economic prosperity.[10] The International Adult Literacy Survey borrows heavily from four of these seminal studies.

The first was the 1985 Young Adult Literacy Survey (YALS) conducted in the United States, which demonstrated the power of the Kirsch–Mosenthal framework as well as the validity and reliability of the measures in a large heterogeneous population. The second was the 1989 Statistics Canada Survey of Literacy Skills Used in Daily Activities (LSUDA). The LSUDA study, conducted in both French and English, showed the feasibility of applying a similar test of literacy independent of cultural and linguistic factors. The third was the DOL Study which was conducted for the U.S. Department of Labor to assess the literacy skills of job seekers in the United States. It was the first U.S. study to employ IALS-type proficiency levels.

The final pertinent study was the 1992 National Adult Literacy Survey (NALS) which, like the YALS, was conducted in the United States. For the NALS study, the U.S. Department of Education financed a massive research initiative to further refine the instruments used to measure the concept of literacy. The IALS capitalized on this by providing a clear psychometric link to the NALS literacy scales.

The IALS framework

The IALS framework is primarily concerned with measuring adult literacy skills, as determined through tested proficiency levels, using stimulus materials drawn from real world applications, found in specific contexts within advanced industrial and post-industrial economies. Each of these elements requires further comment.

The IALS is based on a powerful theory of adult reading, one that links reading difficulty to attributes of the text and the task the reader must perform, and that reflects the use of literacy in everyday life.

Common sense would suggest that literacy is treated as a "cultural given" for most adults in our society. While there are a small number of adults who are unable to read at all, they are usually considered anomalies in the advanced economies. However, the IALS is not really about whether people can read the sentence, "The cat came back." Instead, it is first of all about what adults can measurably do as a result of the sum total of their formal schooling, their formal and informal training, and their application of reading practices and behaviours in daily life. The IALS is based on a powerful theory of adult reading, one that links reading difficulty to attributes of the text and the task the reader must perform, and that reflects the use of literacy in everyday life.

The IALS uses a very complex and sophisticated testing and scaling technology to estimate both item difficulty and proficiency.

Secondly, the IALS is about tested proficiency levels. The IALS uses a very complex and sophisticated testing and scaling technology refined at the Educational Testing Service in Princeton, New Jersey. This scaling technology,[11] which employs Item Response Theory (IRT) to estimate both item difficulty and proficiency, has been successfully used in several international education assessments.

By providing a common yardstick, the IRT-derived proficiency scores provide detailed portraits of the skills of the population. In addition, skill profiles can also be developed for specific subpopulations. So, for instance, the skill levels of those aged 16 to 25 can be compared with those of seniors aged 60 to 69.

The tests used with adults are based on real world applications; they ask the adults tested to work with materials found in everyday life.

Thirdly, the tests used with adults are based on real world applications; they ask the adults tested to work with materials found in everyday life. For instance, the test materials use labels from medicine bottles, simple invoices and receipts,

---

10. Most notably: *Literacy: Profiles of America's Young Adults*, Irwin S. Kirsch and Ann Jungeblut 1986; *Literacy in Canada: a research report*, The Creative Research Group 1987; *Adult Literacy in Canada: Results of a National Study*, Statistics Canada 1991; *Beyond the School Doors: The Literacy Needs of Job Seekers Served by the U.S. Department of Labor*, Kirsch et al. 1992; *Adult Literacy in America: A First Look at the Results of the National Adult Literacy Survey*, Kirsch et al. 1993.

11. See details in Appendix B.

materials that provide directions to assemble things, transportation maps, prose articles from newspapers and magazines, and items that require very simple mathematical calculations.[12]

Objectively speaking, few of the items used in the IALS were very difficult, but the items differ significantly from casual or pleasure reading in that they all involve locating and working with specific pieces of information in order to provide a correct answer. One would hope, for instance, that a person reading a medicine bottle label would be able to determine the proper maximum daily dosage, but when tested, a surprising number of adults failed to get the correct answer.

The unique value of the IALS test items comes, however, from their collective capacity to predict, with a high degree of certainty, whether a respondent would be able to handle unfamiliar texts with similar attributes of difficulty. It is this predictability of the unfamiliar that makes literacy such a strategic asset for both individuals and nations, one that allows both to innovate, adapt and learn.

The unique value of the IALS test items comes, however, from their collective capacity to predict, with a high degree of certainty, whether a respondent would be able to handle unfamiliar texts with similar attributes of difficulty. It is this predictability of the unfamiliar that makes literacy such a strategic asset for both individuals and nations, one that allows both to innovate, adapt and learn.

In keeping with its role as a test of adult literacy skill, IALS deals *both* with text and print decoding skills, *and* with decision skills. To be placed at a particular level, respondents have to consistently perform tasks correctly at that level. The threshold for consistent performance was set at 80%.

So, the IALS does not challenge the reality that most adults can in fact read, but it does question whether they can read well enough to get the correct answers on test items that represent the range of difficulty found in tasks that they encounter in their daily lives. The ability to carefully and critically read printed materials while looking for key pieces of information is a highly prized workplace skill, and the IALS calls into question the very meaning of a "literate adult" in modern society.

This final point, that the IALS is about literacy in the advanced industrial or post-industrial societies, also bears comment. The IALS is concerned with the rapid social and economic change that is affecting all OECD countries.[13]

As our industrial economy evolves into a post-industrial professional services and information economy, the demand for high level literacy skills will most likely rise accordingly. Agrarian society was less information-intensive than industrial society, and the skill needs were correspondingly lower. In agrarian society, high-level literates were primarily clustered in the professions. In turn, industrialism had lower literacy skill requirements than is the case today.

We know that literacy demands in the information economy are rising, even if our understanding of this rising demand is based on qualitative and conjectural evidence. Modern life is faster, with more printed—and electronic—materials being put before us daily than ever before, and our daily decisions are much more likely to involve the use of print. This was not the case even a decade ago.

Perhaps, when all is said and done, we may need another word to describe what we have labeled "literacy skills." Some have suggested the term "adult critical reading skills," and this does seem to offer some added value. For the moment, "literacy skills" will have to suffice; but the IALS and other similar studies do force a reconceptualization of our common-sense understanding of what literacy means. Adult literacy today means adults reading instructions on how to use a new piece of equipment at work, looking at labels on hazardous waste containers, following directions for assembling Christmas toys, reading software manuals, or scanning a computer screen while doing their banking.

---

12. See details in Appendix B.

13. "Transitions to learning economies and societies," in *Lifelong Learning for All*, OECD 1996.

Survey administration

The IALS was conducted in homes by experienced interviewers who administered the literacy tasks in a neutral, non-threatening manner. The survey design combined educational testing techniques with those of household survey research to measure literacy and to provide the information necessary to make these measures meaningful. Respondents were first asked a series of questions to obtain background and demographic information on educational attainment, literacy practices at work and at home, labour force information, adult education participation and literacy self-assessment.

Once this questionnaire was completed, the interviewer presented a booklet containing six simple tasks. If the respondent failed to complete at least two of these correctly, the interview was adjourned. Respondents who completed two or more tasks correctly were given a much larger variety of tasks, drawn from a pool of 114 items, in a separate booklet. These tests were not timed and respondents were urged to try each exercise. Respondents were given maximum leeway to demonstrate their skill levels, even if their measured skills were minimal.

Literacy, as understood in the IALS and in this report, is not a simple dichotomy that distinguishes those who have it from those who do not. Rather, it is a continuous distribution of abilities that depends on the type of information and the complexity of the tasks presented. This understanding of literacy recognizes that *everyone* has some level of literacy skill and proficiency.

The results of the International Adult Literacy Survey were reported using three measures or scale dimensions—prose, document and quantitative—instead of a single measure. The proficiency scores for each scale ranged from 0 to 500, with 0 representing the lowest ability. Each scale was then grouped into five empirically determined literacy levels.[14]

Figure I.1 demonstrates the scale range and illustrates the numerical scale values that define each of the five levels. These values are the same for all three scales. In addition, Figure I.2 provides a summary of the scale score ranges and sample tasks for each of the three literacy domains: prose, document and quantitative.

Literacy in the IALS is not a simple dichotomy that distinguishes those who have it from those who do not. The IALS recognizes that everyone has some level of literacy skill and proficiency.

The IALS reported on three literacy domains—prose, document and quantitative—instead of a single measure. The proficiency scores for each scale ranged from 0 to 500, with 0 representing the lowest ability. Each scale was then grouped into five empirically determined literacy levels.

Figure I.1
IRT scale: Range and skill level values

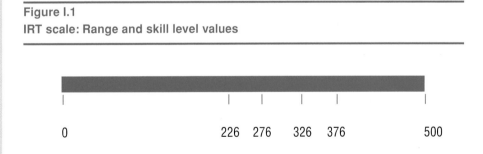

0   226   276   326   376   500

Level 1   Level 2   Level 3   Level 4   Level 5

---

14. For purposes of this report, Levels 4 and 5 on each scale, which represent advanced skills, were collapsed into one composite Level 4/5.

Figure I.2

Scale score ranges and task samples

Level	Score	Prose	Document	Quantitative
1	0–225	Use the instructions on the bottle to identify the maximum duration recommended for taking aspirin.	Identify the percentage of Greek teachers who are women by looking at a simple pictorial graph.	Fill in the figure on the last line of an order form, "Total with Handling," by adding the ticket price of $50 to a handling charge of $2.
2	226–275	Identify a short piece of information about the characteristics of a garden plant, from a written article.	Identify the year in which the fewest Dutch people were injured by fireworks, when presented with two simple graphs.	Work out how many degrees warmer today's forecast high temperature is in Bangkok than in Seoul, using a table accompanying a weather chart.
3	276–325	State which of a set of four movie reviews was the least favourable.	Identify the time of the last bus on a Saturday night, using a bus schedule.	Work out how much more energy Canada produces than it consumes, by comparing figures on two bar charts.
4	326–375	Answer a brief question on how to conduct a job interview, requiring the reader to read a pamphlet on recruitment interviews and integrate two pieces of information into a single statement.	Summarize how the percentages of oil used for different purposes changed over a specified period, by comparing two pie charts.	Calculate how much money you will have if you invest $100 at a rate of 6% for 10 years, using a compound interest table.
5	376–500	Use an announcement from a personnel department to answer a question that uses different phrasing from that used in the text.	Identify the average advertised price for the best-rated basic clock radio in a consumer survey, requiring the assimilation of several pieces of information.	Use information on a table of nutritional analysis to calculate the percentage of calories in a Big Mac® that comes from total fat.

The five IALS proficiency levels were based on qualitative shifts in the skills and strategies required to succeed at various tasks along the scales, ranging from simple to complex.

The five IALS proficiency levels were based on qualitative shifts in the skills and strategies required to succeed at various tasks along the scales, ranging from simple to complex.[15] This scaling method gives a more detailed picture of the distance between successive levels of information-processing skills, and allows analysis based on performance for a broad array of reading tasks.

15. See details in Appendix B.

Sample size and limitations

The primary objective of the IALS study was to compare national Canadian literacy profiles with those of several of Canada's key trading partners. As the data presented in *Literacy, Economy and Society: Results of the first International Adult Literacy Survey* (Organisation for Economic Co-operation and Development and Statistics Canada 1995) so amply demonstrate, the comparative dimension allows a unique understanding of the determinants of the literacy skill profiles and, more importantly, how they can be shaped by thoughtful public policy. Given the social and economic determinants at play, the basic literacy profile is unlikely to have changed significantly in the five years between the LSUDA survey and the IALS.

The Canadian sample was also designed to produce estimates for several specific subpopulations of particular interest to policy makers: in-school youth (aged 16 to 24, in school full time); out-of-school youth (aged 16 to 24, not in school full time); residents of Ontario whose mother tongue is French and who still understand French; residents of New Brunswick who answered the task booklets in French; seniors (aged 65 and over); and social assistance recipients and Unemployment Insurance beneficiaries. Table I.1 provides details of the distribution of the sample geographically, while Table I.2 offers the same for several age groups.

Table I.1

IALS sample size by region

Region	Sample size	Population aged 16 and over
Atlantic provinces[1]	1,535	1,786,424
Quebec	794	5,431,033
Ontario	1,925	8,004,546
Western provinces[2]	1,406	6,085,890
Canada	5,660	21,307,893

1. New Brunswick, Newfoundland, Nova Scotia and Prince Edward Island.

2. Alberta, British Columbia, Manitoba and Saskatchewan.

Table I.2

IALS sample size by age group

Age group	Sample size	Population aged 16 and over
16 to 24	1,193	3,369,904
25 to 44	2,006	9,080,575
45 to 64	1,212	5,749,886
65 and over	1,249	3,107,529
Canada	5,660	21,307,893

Note: Numbers may not add due to rounding.

The basic sample is proportional to population for all provinces and regions. Table I.1 shows that oversampling for specific subpopulations has boosted the sample yield in the Atlantic provinces and Ontario. Other than New Brunswick (which sponsored an enhanced sample), only Quebec and Ontario have populations large enough to support estimates within the limits of the IALS sample size.[16]

Many readers may question the lack of estimates for some provinces. All were offered an opportunity to purchase additional sample, but only three—Alberta, Ontario and New Brunswick—chose to do so.

---

16. The samples for Alberta and British Columbia allow only for univariate estimates of proficiency. More detailed analysis is not possible without resorting to complex, multivariate techniques.

The main study sample was drawn from the Labour Force Survey frame. As a result, it excludes residents of the Northwest Territories and Yukon, inmates of institutions, persons living on Indian reserves and full-time members of the Canadian Armed Forces. Although the survey included data on Aboriginal Canadians living off reserves, the estimates are too small to permit separate analysis.

Any survey is constrained by costs, sample size, study design and objectives. Certain important issues in literacy, such as family literacy practices, have not, for instance, been explored in this report for lack of either data or space. However, as the next chapters demonstrate, it still provides a rich understanding of the role and place of this key human capital skill in Canada's future.

NOTE TO READERS

Most of the discussion in the balance of this report concerns the literacy of all Canadians, aged 16 and over. The need to make comparisons with the LSUDA data and other IALS countries, however, means that only part of the adult population is represented in some tables and graphs. For example, because the LSUDA survey did not include those over age 69, comparison with LSUDA data can be based only on the IALS 16-to-69 subpopulation. Because several IALS countries did not collect data from those over 65, international comparisons are even more restricted, including only those Canadians aged 16 to 65. Some results are appropriate only for part of the population; for example, those concerning reading at work naturally include only information on Canadians in the labour force. Standardizing the age range allows comparisons to be legitimate. Readers are, however, cautioned to carefully note the ages covered in each table and graph.

In general, results from all three scales are reported in tables in this report. While there is a close relationship overall between the three scales, individuals do not necessarily perform equally well on each scale. However, some tables and graphs may include only one scale where the pattern of results is similar across scales. Also, for reasons of clarity, the estimates in this report exclude respondents who either refused to answer a question, did not know the answer, or otherwise did not provide an answer. The effect on distributions is negligible, and does not in any way affect the observed relationships. Estimates may not add to 100% due to rounding.

Generally this report provides a largely descriptive summary of the Canadian data from the IALS. There is no attempt to document all the relationships that might be explored using the IALS data—that would make for a prohibitively large report—but rather to point to important findings. A series of more narrowly focused analytic studies will follow, with more detailed investigations of particular questions.

Statistics Canada – Catalogue no. 89-551-XPE

Chapter 1

Demographic distributions of literacy in Canada

Stan Jones
Consultant in Adult Literacy and Adult Education

While there is new information in the IALS, the fundamental story remains the same: significant numbers of adult Canadians have low literacy skills that constrain their economic and social participation.

As the Introduction to this report makes clear, the IALS was not intended to be a wholly new and different survey of literacy in Canada. It was, rather, to be an extension of the LSUDA study, one that sought to answer some of the policy issues raised in the first study. While there is new information in the IALS, the fundamental story remains the same: significant numbers of adult Canadians have low literacy skills that constrain their economic and social participation.

The regional distribution of literacy

At the broad national level, the IALS findings are consistent with those of the LSUDA study: there is considerable variation in Canadians' literacy skills and that variation differs by region. Generally, there are larger numbers of adults with high skill levels in the western provinces,[1] and larger numbers with low skills in the east (Table 1.1).

Readers should note that the levels of literacy presented in Table 1.1 differ from those defined for the LSUDA study. In the IALS the lowest level, Level 1, is analytically equivalent to LSUDA Levels 1 and 2.[2] This change was based on analysis of the LSUDA data and similar data from the United States, which suggested that there was little need to distinguish between the two lowest LSUDA levels. The same analysis suggested a need to provide more levels at the higher end of each literacy scale. Thus, the IALS replaces the highest LSUDA level, Level 4, with three new levels—3, 4 and 5—as shown below.

Comparison of proficiency levels between the 1989 Survey of Literacy Skills Used in Daily Activities and the 1994 International Adult Literacy Survey

LSUDA proficiency level	IALS proficiency level
0[3]	1
1	1
2	1
3	2
4	3, 4, 5

---

1. Because of the limitations of sample size it is not possible to present separate estimates for Newfoundland, Nova Scotia, Prince Edward Island, Manitoba and Saskatchewan. Readers are cautioned that sample size limitations mean that the sampling variability of the estimates in the other provinces is large, and that the numbers must be interpreted with caution.

2. See Appendix B for a description of the levels.

3. In the LSUDA survey, individuals who were unwilling or unable to be tested were placed in LSUDA Level 0. Following the practice adopted in earlier U.S. studies, the IALS includes such individuals in the proficiency estimates. See *Estimating Literacy Proficiencies With and Without Cognitive Data*, Kentaro Yamamoto and Irwin S. Kirsch 1993 for a detailed discussion of the rationale underlying this decision.

Table 1.1

The distribution of literacy skills on three scales by region and selected provinces of Canada, adults aged 16 and over

| | Prose scale | | | |
| | Level | | | |
	1	2	3	4/5
	%			
Canada	22	26	33	20
Atlantic provinces[1]	25	26	35	15
New Brunswick	28	31	25	16
Quebec	28	26	39	8
Ontario	19	28	28	25
Western provinces[2]	18	24	34	25
Alberta	15	21	36	29
British Columbia	19	24	35	22

| | Document scale | | | |
| | Level | | | |
	1	2	3	4/5
	%			
Canada	23	24	30	22
Atlantic provinces[1]	28	26	32	14
New Brunswick	29	30	24	16
Quebec	31	27	29	13
Ontario	21	22	31	26
Western provinces[2]	19	25	29	27
Alberta	16	21	33	30
British Columbia	20	29	27	25

| | Quantitative scale | | | |
| | Level | | | |
	1	2	3	4/5
	%			
Canada	22	26	32	20
Atlantic provinces[1]	23	30	30	16
New Brunswick	25	34	27	14
Quebec	28	32	30	10
Ontario	20	23	34	23
Western provinces[2]	18	24	33	25
Alberta	13	22	38	27
British Columbia	21	23	34	23

1. New Brunswick, Newfoundland, Nova Scotia and Prince Edward Island.

2. Alberta, British Columbia, Manitoba and Saskatchewan.

Western Canada and Ontario generally have higher literacy skills than Atlantic Canada and Quebec. The distribution of literacy is related to the distribution of educational attainment, but is not identical to it.

Once analysis of the IALS data began, however, it became clear that there was such a small proportion of the population at the highest level (Level 5), particularly when comparisons between groups were being made, that the distinction between Levels 4 and 5 could not be supported with the available sample size. The IALS tables presented in this report, therefore, combined these levels to ensure the statistical reliability of results. In some cases, the average scores, rather than levels, are used when this perspective provides a better picture of the relation of literacy to other characteristics.

Readers will also note that the IALS distinguished between two kinds of reading: that concerned with typical texts (newspapers, books and manuals, for example), referred to in the IALS as prose literacy, and that concerned with texts that depend on layout and graphics (forms, maps, tables and graphs), referred to as document literacy. Studies have shown the importance of decomposing the LSUDA reading scale in this way. The IALS also reports on quantitative literacy, which is concerned with arithmetic operations. In the LSUDA, quantitative literacy was referred to as numeracy.

Changes in literacy: IALS and LSUDA compared

As noted earlier, given the social and economic determinants at play, the basic literacy profile is unlikely to have changed significantly in the five years since the LSUDA study.

Table 1.2 presents an approximate comparison of the national results between the IALS and the LSUDA survey. The differences between the two studies are not large, suggesting that the LSUDA findings still remain valid at the level of relationships. The differences that do exist, which are of little statistical or practical significance, likely reflect growth in the ability to measure adult literacy more precisely. The IALS data presented in Table 1.2 have been restricted to include only respondents aged 16 to 69 to match the ages covered by the LSUDA survey.

The IALS findings provide little evidence to support some pundits' dire predictions of a rapid erosion of either educational quality, or the adult skill base. Since the LSUDA survey was conducted in 1989, those leaving the labour force have been replaced, by and large, by an incoming cohort of young Canadians who are collectively much better educated and more literate. Thus, one would have expected to observe some improvement in the overall skill distribution.[4] The fact that no appreciable improvement can be detected suggests that other processes are altering the skill base. Such an effect should concern policy makers, and needs to be the subject of a detailed and thorough analysis before the underlying economic and social processes driving skill supply are fully understood. The balance of this report points out, however, that both individuals and employers play a key role in skill acquisition and maintenance. This, in turn, raises some interesting questions about what forces drive changes in skill demand in the economy.

LSUDA Levels 1 and 2 cover much the same range of skills as IALS Level 1; LSUDA Level 4 closely matches IALS Levels 3 and 4/5. The distribution is similar in the two studies, except that there are slightly larger proportions at IALS 2 than at LSUDA 3 and, consequently, slightly smaller proportions at IALS 3 and 4/5 than at LSUDA 4. The differences are likely because of the improved measurements used for the IALS.

Table 1.2

Comparisons of the distribution of literacy on the three IALS scales with that on the single LSUDA reading scale, Canadian adults aged 16 to 69

Scale	IALS levels			
	1	2	3	4/5
		%		
Prose	18	26	35	22
Document	19	25	32	24
Quantitative	18	26	34	22

	LSUDA levels			
	1	2	3	4
		%		
LSUDA	7	9	22	62

Canada in context: The international dimension of the IALS

Because the proportions at each level are much the same across the three IALS scales in Canada, it might be thought that they measure the same skills. However, data from other countries in the IALS study suggest otherwise (Table 1.3).[5] The comparative data also provide a useful perspective on the Canadian findings.

---

4. Of the new cohort aged 16 to 20 measured in 1994, only 9% were at Level 1 on the prose scale, 6% were at that level on the document scale, and 8% fell into that range on the quantitative scale; contrast this with the exiting cohort measured in 1989 (now aged 70 to 74), of whom 48% were at Level 1 on the prose and document scales, and 43% were at that level on the quantitative scale.

5. Most of the IALS countries did not collect data from individuals over 65, so the international comparisons are restricted to the 16-to-65 subpopulation.

Table 1.3

The distribution of literacy on the three IALS scales for the countries
participating in the first round, adults aged 16 to 65

	Prose scale			
		Level		
	1	2	3	4/5
		%		
Canada	17	26	35	23
Germany	14	34	38	13
Netherlands	11	30	44	15
Poland	43	35	20	3
Sweden	8	20	40	32
Switzerland (French)	18	34	39	10
Switzerland (German)	19	36	36	9
United States	21	26	32	21

	Document scale			
		Level		
	1	2	3	4/5
		%		
Canada	18	25	32	25
Germany	9	33	40	19
Netherlands	10	26	44	20
Poland	45	31	18	6
Sweden	6	19	39	36
Switzerland (French)	16	29	39	16
Switzerland (German)	18	29	37	16
United States	24	26	31	19

	Quantitative scale			
		Level		
	1	2	3	4/5
		%		
Canada	17	26	35	22
Germany	7	27	43	24
Netherlands	10	26	44	20
Poland	39	30	24	7
Sweden	7	19	39	36
Switzerland (French)	13	25	42	20
Switzerland (German)	14	26	41	19
United States	21	25	31	23

Canada, as does the United States, typically has larger numbers at both the lowest and highest levels, except in comparison with Sweden and Poland, which have quite distinct distributions. The distributions are similar across the scales in most countries, but differ from scale to scale in Germany.

In general, one can describe the distribution of literacy in the IALS countries as follows:

- Estimates for Canada and the United States have quite similar distribution patterns, although there is a slightly larger proportion at Level 1 in the United States. Both countries have relatively large numbers at Level 1 and Level 4/5. The similarity in these distributions suggests that these countries are roughly equal in their economic comparative advantage derived from their literacy profile. This is reassuring given the position of the United States as Canada's most important trading partner. There are larger numbers at Level 1 on the document scale than on the other two scales in both countries. In Canada, there are also larger numbers at Level 4/5 on the document scale than on the prose and quantitative scales.

- In contrast with Canada and the United States, the Netherlands and Germany both show especially large numbers at Level 3, demonstrating that different educational policies can generate quite different literacy outcomes.

- Sweden is characterized by substantial numbers at the higher skill levels on all three scales. Sweden is equally high on a number of variables thought to influence the distribution of literacy, including educational attainment and the actual use of literacy in daily life. These differences, in turn, seem to reflect longstanding Swedish education and labour market policies, which have encouraged continuous education and lifelong learning.

- As discussed later in this chapter, skill differences exist between anglophone and francophone Canadians. In contrast, the two language groups surveyed in Switzerland (French and German) show few differences. There are substantial numbers at Level 3 and even higher numbers at Level 4/5 on the quantitative scale. In this way the Swiss sample populations are similar to those in the Netherlands and Germany.

- Poland, the only non-OECD country in the study, shows stronger than expected performance across all three scales. There are larger proportions at the two highest levels on the quantitative scale. The smaller proportions on the document scale may reflect the historical situation in Poland, as this scale represents a type of literacy likely to be more common in a fully market-oriented society.

In the end, what is interesting is not how countries scored, but the ways in which literacy is related to other socio-economic characteristics. The international report highlighted several interesting differences. This national report, like the other countries' national reports,[6] is intended to pursue those relationships in greater detail using the IALS Canadian data.

Literacy and educational attainment

The differences in the distribution of literacy across Canada are consistent with differences in the distribution of other characteristics of the population that are associated with it. For example, literacy is closely associated with educational attainment (Table 1.4).[7] Since regions of Canada differ greatly in educational attainment, it follows that they would differ in literacy. About 18% of those aged 15 and over in the Atlantic region and 21% of those in Quebec have less than Grade 9 education, but only 12% of Ontarians and 11% of those in the Western provinces have this level of education.[8]

Figure 1.1 compares the average prose score for those with each level of education in the four regions. When differences in educational attainment are held constant, the patterns of differences between regions become regular, suggesting that much of the regional difference found in literacy ability is simply a reflection of the differences in educational attainment. Sweeping generalizations about provincial and regional literacy differences need to be understood in a larger education attainment context.

---

6. Several other countries participating in the IALS plan to publish national reports concurrently with Canada. See, for example, *Adult Literacy: An International Perspective*, U.S. Department of Education 1996.

7. It is, of course, tempting to draw causal relationships, or to "explain" literacy. It is better to avoid strong causal claims. This survey, like all cross-sectional surveys, is only a picture of characteristics that occur together. Because there is no longitudinal element, or any "experimental" design, causal conclusions cannot be drawn. In any case, the causal relationship between literacy and other variables is likely to flow in both directions. It is common to think of education causing literacy, because most people learn to read in school and because school provides the setting for much reading. It is also true, however, that individuals with lower literacy skills are less likely to pursue further education; thus, it is plausible to think that literacy "causes" education. Stanovich (1986) discusses this "Matthew" effect in schooling, pointing out that students who are successful readers are offered more opportunities to read higher quality materials.

8. *Educational attainment and school attendance: The nation (1991 Census)*, Statistics Canada 1993.

Table 1.4

The distribution of literacy on each of three scales by highest level of educational attainment, Canadian adults aged 16 and over

There is a strong relationship between education and literacy level on all three scales: the correlation for prose and education is .60, for document and education .57, and for quantitative and education .63. Statistically, one can interpret these correlations as suggesting that education "accounts" for just over one-third of the variation in literacy. That means that considerable variation is related to other factors. Secondary school graduates and those completing community college do better on the document scale than on the prose or quantitative scales, while those completing university perform better on prose and quantitative than on document.

	Prose scale			
		Level		
Highest level of education	1	2	3	4/5
		%		
Less than Grade 8	89	9	...	...
Completed primary school	59	29	12	...
Some secondary school	25	36	32	7
Secondary school graduate	12	31	40	18
Community college graduate	7	23	45	25
University graduate	...	11	33	56

	Document scale			
		Level		
Highest level of education	1	2	3	4/5
		%		
Less than Grade 8	92	6	...	...
Completed primary school	65	21	13	...
Some secondary school	27	39	25	9
Secondary school graduate	13	29	36	22
Community college graduate	7	18	39	36
University graduate	...	11	40	46

	Quantitative scale			
		Level		
Highest level of education	1	2	3	4/5
		%		
Less than Grade 8	91	8	...	...
Completed primary school	61	25	14	...
Some secondary school	26	41	26	7
Secondary school graduate	11	33	41	16
Community college graduate	7	22	46	25
University graduate	...	5	33	60

...   Sample size too small to produce reliable estimates.

What is the relationship between educational attainment and literacy? The IALS does not provide any direct information on what a "minimally desirable" level of literacy might be, although it is clear that individuals at Level 1 must find dealing with print difficult. The number of Canadians who have at least completed secondary school and are at Level 1 is small: fewer than 10% of secondary school graduates are at this level. It is possible to identify some typical configurations of literacy by education attainment.

Figure 1.1

Average prose score by educational attainment for each region of Canada, adults aged 16 and over

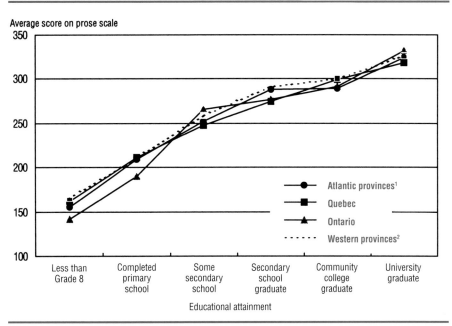

Average score on prose scale

Although the regions differ overall in the distribution of literacy, the differences appear to be simply a function of different educational attainment in the regions. When the comparisons are made within levels of educational attainment, there are no systematic regional differences.

1. New Brunswick, Newfoundland, Nova Scotia and Prince Edward Island.

2. Alberta, British Columbia, Manitoba and Saskatchewan.

Highest level of educational attainment	Typical literacy pattern
No secondary education	Most at Level 1, particularly those who have not completed primary school; only very few individuals at Level 4/5.
Some secondary school	Largest number at Level 2; representation at Levels 1 and 3.
Secondary school graduate	Largest number at Level 3; second largest at Level 2.
Community college graduate	Largest number at Level 3; second largest at Level 4/5.
University graduate	Largest number at Level 4/5; a handful of individuals at Level 1.

Another way of looking at the relationship between education and literacy are the box plots in Figure 1.2. The "box" part of each plot encloses the middle of the distribution of scores, with the horizontal bar positioned at the mean. The "whiskers" extend from the box to represent the standard range of scores. The plots clearly demonstrate the increase in mean scores with increased education. They also indicate that the gain in literacy moving from secondary graduate to postsecondary graduate is not as large as that moving from less than secondary graduate to secondary graduate.

Figure 1.2

Box plots of the distribution of scores for each literacy scale by educational attainment

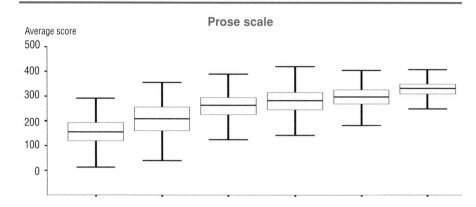

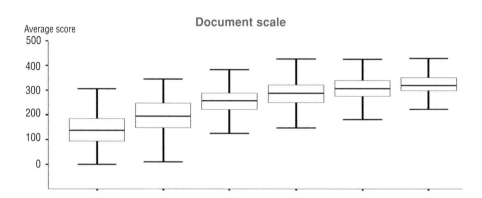

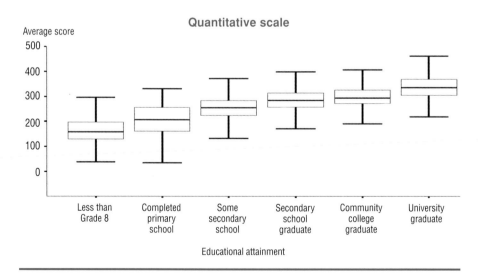

As education increases, so does the mean and the central range of scores. Education appears to have the greatest effect on prose and quantitative scale scores. This is consistent with the observation that document scale tasks are least covered in school.

While the relationship between literacy and education is strong, it is far from perfect.

While the relationship between literacy and education is strong, it is far from perfect. Many individuals did not fit the general pattern. One-third of Canadians who had not completed secondary school were at Level 3 or above; a quarter or more of those who had completed a community college program were at Level 1 or 2. In all, some 20% of the IALS sample population had literacy levels lower than the statistical model would predict, and some 16% had literacy levels higher than the model; therefore, over one-third of the population did not fit the assumed pattern.

Thus, education does not "fix" literacy forever. Individuals can lose skills after the end of schooling, through lack of use, or they can gain skills, through practice and additional training, even with minimal formal education. That literacy is not a skill fixed by education is important to literacy policy in Canada: it makes it clear that literacy can be influenced by what people choose to do after leaving school. It also makes it imperative that literacy policies be based on a clear understanding of how skills are both lost and gained in adulthood. Also key are the practices of literacy in adult life, which, in turn, make the sort of analysis of these practices that is presented in Chapter 3 an essential component of literacy research.

The pattern of the relationship of literacy to educational attainment in Canada is similar to that in the United States, but differs from that in Germany in interesting ways (Table 1.5).

Table 1.5

Comparisons of the relation between educational attainment and literacy for three countries across the three literacy scales, adults aged 16 to 65

		Scale		
		Prose	Document	Quantitative
			%	
Proportion of population aged	Canada	68	74	69
16 to 65 with less than secondary	Germany	68	56	43
education who are at Level 1	United States	69	74	67
Proportion of population aged	Canada	20	24	17
16 to 65 with secondary education	Germany	14	25	26
only who are at Level 4/5	United States	14	13	15

In Canada and the United States, there are roughly consistent patterns of the distribution of literacy by education across the three scales; however, this is not the case in Germany. Although all three countries had similar proportions of those with low education at Level 1 on the prose scale, there were smaller proportions at Level 1 on the document and quantitative scales in Germany.[9] Although the differences were not as great for those who had completed only secondary school, there was a tendency in Germany for a larger proportion at higher levels on the document and quantitative scales compared with prose, while in Canada and the United States the proportions on the three scales were similar, with Canada showing more variation than the United States.

Differences in literacy practices of German adults and the stronger emphasis on work-related experiences that characterizes the German dual system for secondary school–vocational education may contribute to these differences.[10] The IALS results indicate that document and quantitative skills are particularly important to workplace success. If this is the case, then these results suggest that German young adults may be better prepared for work-related literacy than their North American counterparts, an effect linked to educational and labour market policy.

Among Canadian adults who have only a secondary school education, those who took vocational programs did not do as well as those who took academic programs (Table 1.6). While it may be that those who chose the vocational route were those with lower skills at the start of secondary school, their school experience did not provide them with the same level of skill as did the education received by their German counterparts. These results lend support to policy options that aim

---

9.   Germany is exceptional in the IALS in this regard. In all the other IALS countries, the pattern was similar to that in Canada and the United States.

10.   Document and quantitative tasks of the kind assessed in the IALS are less likely to occur in educational settings than are the prose tasks.

to increase the work experience of Canadian secondary students through co-op programs, apprenticeships, and other school-to-work arrangements.

Table 1.6

The distribution of literacy for each of three types of secondary school programs, Canadian adults aged 16 and over whose highest educational attainment is secondary school graduation

| | Prose scale | | | |
| | | Level | | |
Type of secondary program	1	2	3	4/5
		%		
Academic	9	30	41	20
Business/Vocational	15	30	38	17
Equivalency	...	41	33	...

| | Document scale | | | |
| | | Level | | |
Type of secondary program	1	2	3	4/5
		%		
Academic	10	23	40	28
Business/Vocational	16	41	27	17
Equivalency	16	30	42	...

| | Quantitative scale | | | |
| | | Level | | |
Type of secondary program	1	2	3	4/5
		%		
Academic	9	25	47	20
Business/Vocational	10	41	38	11
Equivalency	...	47	26	...

...   Sample size too small to produce reliable estimates.

Those who took an academic program are more likely to be in a higher level than those who were in a business program or who took an equivalency program. The differences are particularly noticeable on the document scale. It is not possible to assign any causal relationship because individuals may have selected (or had selected for them) their secondary school program based on their literacy skills.

One way of more directly assessing the impact of education on literacy is to look at young adults who have had little opportunity to acquire (or lose) skill through workplace activities. Table 1.7 presents the distribution of literacy for respondents aged 16 to 20, categorized by their educational attainment using categories taken from the School Leavers Survey: graduates are those who have completed secondary school, continuers are those who are still in secondary school, and leavers are those who did not complete secondary school.[11]

Those who have left school without a secondary school diploma have lower skills than those who have graduated. These results portray one of the tangible consequences of leaving school early, consequences that carry with them significant lifetime social and economic costs.

Clearly those who left school without a secondary school diploma had lower skills than those who graduated. These results portray one of the tangible consequences of leaving school early, consequences that carry with them significant lifetime social and economic costs. While secondary school graduates were naturally slightly older (less than 20% of them were under 18), the age difference was less than a year (average age for graduates was 18.8; for leavers, 17.9). Most of the graduates, however, had postsecondary education (63% were in college or university and 18% had completed a college program). This undoubtedly contributed to their higher score. The greatest differences between continuers and graduates was on the document scale. School provides less structured experience with documents than with prose or quantitative tasks, and this may contribute to the greater effect life experience has on this scale.

11. *Leaving school: results from a national survey comparing school leavers and high school graduates 18 to 20 years of age*, Statistics Canada 1993. The age range, 20 and under, was taken to be consistent with school leavers, although the group considered here includes 16- and 17-year-olds; these were not included in the school leavers group. That study also had a fourth category, for those not currently in school with less than Grade 8; there was only one IALS respondent in the Canadian sample who fit this description, and this individual has been grouped with the other leavers.

Table 1.7

The distribution of literacy by current school status, Canadian adults aged 16 to 20

| | Prose scale | | | |
| | | Level | | |
School status	1	2	3	4/5
		%		
Graduates	...	24	47	27
Continuers	16	27	43	14
Leavers	...	48	...	...

| | Document scale | | | |
| | | Level | | |
School status	1	2	3	4/5
		%		
Graduates	...	15	33	50
Continuers	...	37	37	18
Leavers	...	43	...	...

| | Quantitative scale | | | |
| | | Level | | |
School status	1	2	3	4/5
		%		
Graduates	...	22	59	16
Continuers	9	42	37	13
Leavers	...	41	...	...

...   Sample size too small to produce reliable estimates.

As expected, those who have completed secondary school (graduates) are more likely to have high literacy skills than the leavers (those not in school who do not have a diploma). Also as expected, those still in secondary school (continuers) do not have as large a proportion at high levels as the graduates, but outperform the leavers.

Interestingly, the lower scores of the leavers may have contributed to their decision to leave school without a diploma. Thus, literacy was a determinant of educational attainment as well as a consequence.

     The differences between the continuers and the leavers is not as dramatic as that between graduates and leavers, though those still in school did better than those who left. The continuers had 1.5 more years of education but were younger (average age was 16.5; 60% were only 16 years old), and the greater work experience of the leavers may substitute for some of the additional education. The continuers, despite their younger age, outperformed the leavers. This suggests that the lower scores of the leavers may have contributed to their decision to leave school without a diploma. Thus, literacy was a determinant of educational attainment as well as a consequence. While the School Leavers Survey did not test the skills of its respondents, it did ask them for a self-report of their grades in their last year of school. More than three-quarters (77%) of the graduates had A or B averages, but only 37% of the leavers had averages at these levels. In contrast, 53% of the leavers had averages of C or lower, but only 20% of the graduates had such low grades.[12]

---

12.   The other 10% of leavers and 3% of graduates did not provide a grade average.

Literacy and gender

Education may play a role, in a different way, in the observed differences between men and women on the IALS scales (Table 1.8). Women scored higher than men on the prose scale (the average score for women was 275; for men, 265),[13] with almost one-quarter scoring at Level 4/5 in contrast with 16% of the men at this level. On the other hand, men scored marginally higher on the quantitative scale (the average score for men was 275; for women, 270)[14] and on the document scale (men, 271; women, 267),[15] although the practical significance of the latter differences is small.

Table 1.8

The distribution of literacy by gender for each scale, Canadian adults aged 16 and over

| | Prose scale | | | |
| | Level | | | |
	1	2	3	4/5
		%		
Women	20	25	31	24
Men	23	27	35	16

| | Document scale | | | |
| | Level | | | |
	1	2	3	4/5
		%		
Women	25	24	30	21
Men	22	25	30	23

| | Quantitative scale | | | |
| | Level | | | |
	1	2	3	4/5
		%		
Women	23	27	33	18
Men	21	25	32	22

Similar male–female differences were found in the CMEC's School Achievement Indicators Program (SAIP) assessments of reading, writing and mathematics among Canadian 13- and 16-year-olds.[16] Girls did notably better than boys in both age groups on the reading and writing assessments, and boys did slightly better than girls on mathematics problem-solving at both ages and on mathematics content at age 16. Other school assessments, such as the National Assessment of Educational Progress in the United States and the international IEA studies,[17] have found similar gender effects. It is not clear why these gender effects exist, though different course patterns may play some role (although this

---

13. $t = 5.69, p < .001$.

14. $t = 2.96, p < .01$.

15. $t = 2.30, p = .02$.

16. *Technical report: Mathematics assessment 1993*, Council of Ministers of Education Canada 1994; *Technical report: Reading and writing assessment*, Council of Ministers of Education Canada 1995.

17. *The International Association for the Evaluation of Educational Achievement (IEA) Study of Reading Literacy: Achievement and Instruction in Thirty-two School Systems*, Warwick B. Elley, ed. 1994.

leaves different patterns unexplained, which may be the result of differential success rather than its cause). The CMEC report provides a nice summary:

> *The causes for these differences in achievement have never been thoroughly explained. While it is often speculated that the differences in performance may be due to differences in maturity levels and in cultural influences between boys and girls, finding the exact causes still presents educational research with a very interesting challenge.*[18]

Whatever the cause, the fact that this effect persists into adulthood should concern educators. Educational attainment in and of itself does not contribute to the gender differences because there are no gender differences in attainment in Canada.

Literacy and language

Another characteristic closely associated with literacy and education is language. Access to education in an individual's preferred language has not always been possible. For example, secondary school education in French became widely available in Ontario and New Brunswick only in the late 1960s. Therefore, for many French-speaking Canadians, the language of their formal studies was not their mother tongue.[19] As a result, the IALS provided respondents with a choice as to which official language they preferred to be tested in.

Table 1.9

Distribution of literacy by language of test, Canadian adults aged 16 and over

| | Prose scale | | | |
| | Level | | | |
	1	2	3	4/5
	%			
English	19	26	31	24
French	28	26	38	9
Quebec	27	25	39	9
Outside Quebec	33	30	25	...

| | Document scale | | | |
| | Level | | | |
	1	2	3	4/5
	%			
English	21	24	31	25
French	31	27	28	14
Quebec	31	27	29	14
Outside Quebec	33	27	25	...

| | Quantitative scale | | | |
| | Level | | | |
	1	2	3	4/5
	%			
English	20	24	33	23
French	28	32	30	10
Quebec	28	32	30	10
Outside Quebec	28	32	29	...

... Sample size too small to produce reliable estimates.

Because educational attainment differs markedly between the language groups, the large differences between the groups seen in this table reflect the historical differential access to education, particularly access to secondary education, in the language of choice in Canada. When educational differences are taken into account, the differences between the language groups no longer show the marked differences (see Figure 1.3).

18. See footnote 16, (p. 99, 1995).

19. Mother tongue, which denotes the language first learned and still understood, sees wide use in Statistics Canada surveys, including the Census of Population. It is perhaps the most inclusive of the definitions of the francophone community in common usage.

The IALS revealed large differences in literacy skill scores between language groups, particularly for francophones living outside Quebec.

Once differences in educational attainment are taken into account, the patterns of inter-language comparison no longer systematically favour one group over the other. This signals that education access, attainment and quality are the main forces driving these literacy differences.

There are overall differences between the language groups, but these are largely a reflection of different educational attainment, itself a result of differential access to secondary and postsecondary education. When the comparisons are made within levels of educational attainment, as in this figure, there are no systematic differences, except that French speakers outside Quebec with postsecondary education, particularly those with college education, are somewhat lower in skill than the other groups.

The results of Table 1.9 and Figure 1.3 are based on the scores of those who took the IALS test in either French or English.[20]

Clearly, as Table 1.9 shows, there are differences in literacy skill scores between language groups. In particular, francophones living outside Quebec who were tested in French had more people at Level 1 on the prose scale. However, these differences tend to disappear on the document and quantitative scales.

In addition, these differences also reflect differences in formal education attainment. Just as with the regional distributions reviewed earlier, once differences in educational attainment are taken into account, the patterns of inter-language comparison no longer systematically favour one group over the other, as Figure 1.3 reveals. This signals that education access, attainment and quality are the main forces driving the literacy differences noted for linguistic minorities.[21]

Figure 1.3

Average prose score by educational attainment for language groups in Canada, adults aged 16 and over

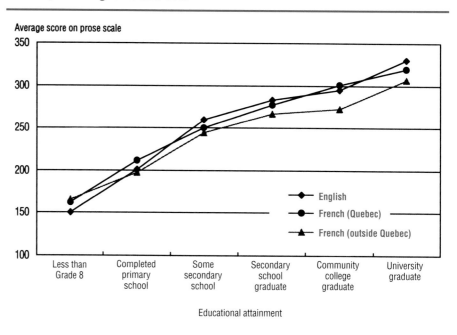

20. Speakers of French have been categorized into two groups, those in Quebec and those outside Quebec. The decision to do so was guided by policy and data. Policies for French speakers outside Quebec are different than for French speakers in that province; for example, increased access to secondary education in French is much more recent for those living outside Quebec. Further, the IALS data show that the average prose scores are significantly different for these two French groups. It is not always clear who is to be included in the group of French speakers. In this report, French results refer to those who chose to answer the test items in French. This does not include all who identified their main language as French; for example, 3% of those who said the language they spoke most easily was French chose to be tested in English.

21. For a detailed analysis of how these forces affect the distribution of literacy in Ontario's francophone population, see *Enquête internationale sur l'alphabétisation des adultes, rapport sur la composante francophone de l'Ontario*, Ontario Ministry of Education and Training (in press).

Table 1.10 distinguishes scale score results for those whose mother tongue was French and took the IALS test in French, from those who took it in English. As Table 1.10 shows, 72% of the respondents who said their mother tongue was French took the test in French. In contrast, 99% of those who said their mother tongue was English took the test in that language. The study does not provide any insight into the French language literacy skills of the 28% of those with French as a mother tongue who chose to be tested in English.

Table 1.10

The distribution of literacy across the three scales by respondent's first language and language of test, Canadian adults aged 16 and over

		Prose scale			
		Level			
First language	Test language	1	2	3	4/5
		%			
English	English (99%)	13	25	35	27
French	Combined	25	27	39	9
	French (72%)	25	27	39	9
	English (28%)	35	23	33	10
Other	Combined	48	26	16	10
	English (96%)	45	28	16	11

		Document scale			
		Level			
First language	Test language	1	2	3	4/5
		%			
English	English (99%)	15	23	35	28
French	Combined	29	27	29	14
	French (72%)	28	28	29	15
	English (28%)	41	22	30	7
Other	Combined	45	25	15	15
	English (96%)	42	26	15	17

		Quantitative scale			
		Level			
First language	Test language	1	2	3	4/5
		%			
English	English (99%)	14	23	37	26
French	Combined	26	32	31	11
	French (72%)	25	32	32	11
	English (28%)	29	34	28	10
Other	Combined	43	26	18	12
	English (96%)	41	26	20	13

Those who reported French as a first language but took the test in English tended to have slightly lower scores as a group than those whose first language and test language were French. Those with French as their first language but who took the English test mostly live in a province other than Quebec or New Brunswick (see Table 1.11).

Various checks were made on where the French mother tongue respondents lived who chose to be tested in English. Most of these people lived in a province other than Quebec or New Brunswick, suggesting how important the cultural and linguistic milieu is for these sorts of choices (Table 1.11).

Table 1.11

Choice of language for test for respondents whose first language is French, by region, Canadian adults aged 16 and over

Region	Language chosen for test	
	French	English
	%	
Atlantic Canada[1] (other than New Brunswick)	...	99
New Brunswick	89	11
Quebec	99	...
Ontario	53	47
Western Canada[2]	...	96

1. Newfoundland, Nova Scotia and Prince Edward Island.

2. Alberta, British Columbia, Manitoba and Saskatchewan.

... Sample size too small to produce reliable estimates.

When other ways in which someone might identify themselves as French in Canada are examined (Table 1.12), around 15% of those who reported using French most often chose to be tested in English. Thus the French results in Table 1.9 represent only part of what might be considered the French-speaking population of Canada. The language of test as the defining criterion for Table 1.9 was chosen because it is the only one that directly ties test results to specific language use.

Table 1.12

Choice of test language by various situations in which French or English was respondent's preference, Canadian adults aged 16 and over

French is:	Language preference	
	Language chosen for test	
	French	English
	%	
First language	72	28
Language used in home	85	15
Language used at work	87	13
Language used in leisure activities	87	13
Language easiest to use	88	12
English is:	English	French
	%	
First language	99	1
Language used in home	97	3
Language used at work	92	8
Language used in leisure activities	96	5
Language easiest to use	97	3

Note: These results are based on unweighted data.

A concern of many observers is with the relative performance of francophone youth. While the overall numbers in the sample for those aged 16 to 25 are not large, we can look at the youth distribution by region. Table 1.13 contains this information; the results for Quebec, where the vast majority of young francophones reside, are quite revealing. Young Quebecers (French and English combined) have a large and significant majority performing at Level 3 on the prose and quantitative scales.

Table 1.13

The distribution of literacy skills on three scales by region, youth aged 16 to 25

	Prose scale			
	Level			
	1	2	3	4/5
	%			
Canada	11	26	44	20
Atlantic provinces[1]	11	32	42	15
Quebec	...	22	56	14
Ontario	17	24	39	21
Western provinces[2]	...	28	41	25

	Document scale			
	Level			
	1	2	3	4/5
	%			
Canada	10	22	36	31
Atlantic provinces[1]	14	29	40	18
Quebec	...	20	40	28
Ontario	...	22	34	32
Western provinces[2]	...	22	36	37

	Quantitative scale			
	Level			
	1	2	3	4/5
	%			
Canada	10	29	45	17
Atlantic provinces[1]	11	34	43	12
Quebec	...	29	54	...
Ontario	13	32	37	18
Western provinces[2]	7	23	47	23

1. New Brunswick, Newfoundland, Nova Scotia and Prince Edward Island.

2. Alberta, British Columbia, Manitoba and Saskatchewan.

... Sample size too small to produce reliable estimates.

A low proportion of the youth cohort are in Level 1, particularly in Quebec and the western provinces, belying claims of widespread school failure. By the same token, few youth reach Level 4/5, which seems to require more exposure to adult life and work activities.

The literacy test scores of francophones appear to be affected greatly by language transfer and milieu. Where the demographics and geographical concentration provide a strong supportive milieu, such as in Quebec and New Brunswick, the scores are higher. When language transfer works its effects, such as among francophones in Western Canada, the scores are lower. The maintenance of strong mother tongue literacy skills appears to depend on high concentrations of people who can tackle language transfer issues, and requires a supportive infrastructure (such as New Brunswick provides) and a receptive cultural milieu.

The maintenance of strong mother tongue literacy skills appears to depend on high concentrations of people who can tackle language transfer issues, and requires a supportive infrastructure and a receptive cultural milieu.

Literacy and immigration

Canadian regions also differ in literacy skill distribution because immigrants[22] are not evenly distributed across the country; more immigrate to Ontario and British Columbia than to other areas. For example, 31% of the Ontario IALS sample and 33% of that in British Columbia were immigrants; Alberta has the third highest proportion, with immigrants making up 21% of the sample. Immigrants are over-represented at both the highest and lowest literacy levels (Table 1.14).

22. Immigrants are defined in this study as those born outside of Canada with no Canadian citizenship and, thus, may include a number of non-permanent residents who have not achieved landed immigrant status.

Table 1.14

Distribution of literacy by immigration status across the three scales, Canadian adults aged 16 and over

| | Prose scale | | | |
| | | Level | | |
Born in Canada?	1	2	3	4/5
		%		
Yes	18	27	37	19
No	36	23	19	22

| | Document scale | | | |
| | | Level | | |
Born in Canada?	1	2	3	4/5
		%		
Yes	20	25	33	21
No	36	21	19	25

| | Quantitative scale | | | |
| | | Level | | |
Born in Canada?	1	2	3	4/5
		%		
Yes	19	28	35	19
No	34	18	24	24

The proportion of immigrants at Level 1 is larger than the proportion of those born in Canada who are at this level. On the other hand, there are also proportionally more immigrants at Level 4/5. Canada is unique in the IALS countries in having such a large proportion of immigrants at the highest level; at the same time, Canada is the only IALS country with a policy favouring the immigration of skilled workers.

No other country studied in the IALS has as large a proportion of immigrants at Level 4/5 as Canada. This presumably reflects the policy of selecting skilled immigrants, which the Canadian government has traditionally followed.

Immigrants in other IALS countries, including the United States, are predominately at Level 1; no other country studied in the IALS has as large a proportion of immigrants at Level 4/5 as Canada. This presumably reflects the policy of selecting skilled immigrants that the Canadian government has traditionally followed. Despite Canada's success in recruiting skilled people, it must also be noted that large numbers of immigrants are at Level 1, reflecting the fact that Canada has also accepted large numbers of immigrants on humanitarian grounds. Changes to the national second-language education policy for immigrants, which are designed to improve the language proficiency of this group, are too recent to have been reflected in the IALS results.

Literacy and age

The most recent school-leaving cohort, aged 16 to 25, contains relatively few individuals at Level 1, and most at Levels 2 and 3, a finding that belies any notion of widespread school failure.

Table 1.15 sets out the distribution of literacy by age and this is what we find: the most recent school-leaving cohort, aged 16 to 25, contains relatively few individuals at Level 1, with most at Levels 2 and 3, a finding that belies any notion of widespread school failure (at least if one is willing to accept that Level 3 is a reasonable threshold). Because younger adults are more likely to have higher levels of educational attainment, it should be expected that they would have higher levels of literacy as well.

In general, larger proportions are found at literacy Level 1 among older groups, paralleling the increase in the proportion with less than secondary education. However, there is no corresponding increase in the proportion at Level 4/5 at younger ages. Only on the document scale is the proportion of the youngest age group (16 to 25) at Level 4/5 as large as the proportion of those aged 26 to 35 and of those aged 36 to 45. That the Level 4/5 proportion of those 16 to 25 is smaller may be attributable to the fact that few Canadians of this age, only 5%, had completed their university studies, while 16% of those 26 to 35 and 17% of those 36 to 45 had done so. The different Level 4/5 proportions for those aged 26 to 35 and 36 to 45 are more likely to reflect the greater work experience of the older age group.

Table 1.15

Distribution of literacy by age across the three scales, Canadian adults aged 16 and over

| | Prose scale | | | |
| | | Level | | |
Age group	1	2	3	4/5
		%		
16 to 25	11	26	44	20
26 to 35	12	29	33	26
36 to 45	13	19	37	31
46 to 55	21	30	31	18
56 to 65	38	26	28	8
Over 65	53	27	19	...

| | Document scale | | | |
| | | Level | | |
Age group	1	2	3	4/5
		%		
16 to 25	10	22	36	31
26 to 35	14	25	34	28
36 to 45	14	22	37	27
46 to 55	23	31	24	22
56 to 65	44	24	24	...
Over 65	58	22	18	...

| | Quantitative scale | | | |
| | | Level | | |
Age group	1	2	3	4/5
		%		
16 to 25	10	29	45	17
26 to 35	12	26	35	28
36 to 45	12	22	36	30
46 to 55	24	32	25	19
56 to 65	40	22	31	7
Over 65	53	27	16	...

... Sample size too small to produce reliable estimates.

The youngest three age groups, those 16 to 45, have a relatively small proportion at Level 1, reflecting their generally high educational attainment. The youngest age group, 16 to 25, has smaller proportions on the prose and quantitative scales than the next two older groups. These are the two scales most closely related to education, suggesting that the difference is due primarily to the fact that many in this age group have not yet completed their education. The two oldest age groups, those over 55, have small proportions at Level 4/5 and large proportions at Level 1, pointing to the lower levels of educational attainment in this population and to the need for literacy services for older Canadians.

Prose and quantitative skills seem more closely related to school experience than do document skills. This fact poses serious concerns for chronically unemployed youth, who will not generally get the focused exposure required to move them to Level 4/5 on the document scale.

Even when educational differences are taken into account one observes a small deterioration in skill with age, a fact that may be related to seniors' dependence on others to cope with the literacy activities of daily living.

That there are different relations of age to skill for different scales provides still further indication that the scales do measure different aspects of skill. In general, prose and quantitative skills seem more closely related to school experience than do document skills, as might be expected because students have less exposure, particularly focused exposure, to document-based tasks in school. This fact poses serious concerns for chronically unemployed youth, who will not generally get the focused exposure required to move them to Level 4/5 on the document scale.

There is a marked difference in literacy between those who were educated primarily after the Second World War and those whose education was completed before or disrupted by that war. In large part this represents significant differences in educational attainment. About 40% of Canadians over 65 have not completed primary school, compared with only 4% of Canadians aged 26 to 35. Just 13% of Canadians 56 to 65 years old have attended university, while 28% of those aged 36 to 45 and 22% of those aged 46 to 55 have done so.[23] Yet even when educational differences are taken into account one observes a small deterioration in skill with age. The correlations range from -.22 for the quantitative scale to -.30 for the prose scale.[24] The small size of the observed decrease in skill is in keeping with the literature, which argues that the effects of aging do not begin to have a serious impact on literacy performance until late in life.[25]

23. See footnote 8.

24. The correlations are negative because as age increases, literacy scores tend to decrease.

25. See for example, "Definitions and Taxonomy of Foundation Skills and Adult Competences: Life Span Perspectives," Jacquie Smith and Michael Marsiske in *Adult Basic Skills: Innovations in Measurement and Policy Analysis* 1996.

As the negative correlations indicate, older Canadians have lower skills than might be suggested by their educational attainment. The consequences of low literacy for Canadian seniors have been explored in a number of studies.[26] Seniors with low literacy skills are restricted in their activities and often depend on others to cope with the literacy activities of daily living. And the actual numbers are large; more than 1.6 million adults over 65 are at Level 1. That low skills do affect seniors' literacy activities is further documented in the analysis of daily practices presented in the next chapter.

Jobs differ in the skills they require: both the generic skills such as literacy and the specific, occupation-related skills. The next chapter also sets out how jobs differ in literacy requirements and the consequences of the literacy demands of the workplace.

---

26. *Something for Seniors: Evaluation report 3 on an adult literacy program for seniors*, Trudy Lothian 1992; *Something Special for Seniors: Evaluation report 1 on an adult literacy program for seniors*, Trudy Lothian and Stan Jones 1991.

Chapter 2

Economic dimensions of literacy in Canada

Stan Jones
Consultant in Adult Literacy and Adult Education

The IALS data clearly show that individuals differ systematically in literacy skills, as does the data from the LSUDA that preceded it. Those differences matter if they lead to different consequences for individuals and nations—and they do. Individuals with low literacy skills find it more difficult to use printed information, they participate less frequently in community activities, and they are less likely to achieve economic success than those with higher skills.

The emerging global economy is characterized by greatly increased flows of information and financial capital. In addition, the reintegration of the Central and Eastern European countries into the world economy, and the continuing rapid advance of industrialized countries in Asia and Latin America, have upset the economic status quo. The economies of the OECD countries now face a large, well-educated and relatively low-wage labour force. While new forms of co-operation across borders have emerged, competition for investment capital has intensified. New opportunities—as well as uncertainties and risks—are inherent in this situation. Certain countries, firms and individuals are well positioned to compete successfully in global markets; others may have difficulty taking advantage of the opportunities. A massive reallocation of labour is expected to occur as countries try to adapt and maintain their economic position.

One of the best prescriptions to exploit the new economic environment is to strengthen the capacity of firms and labour markets to adjust to change, improve their productivity and capitalize on innovation. But this capacity depends first and foremost on the knowledge and skills of the population. Literacy, then, will be a powerful determinant of Canada's innovative and adaptive capacity, and hence our future economic prosperity.

An individual's connection to the world of work is through a job, and different jobs require different skills—both in kind and degree. Therefore, different constellations of skills in different occupations are expected. And jobs differentially promote literacy because some provide opportunities to use literacy skills while others do not.

Literacy and occupations

Changes in the distribution of occupations reflect the transformation that is occurring as Canada moves from an industrial to an information economy. These changes carry important consequences that will determine how Canada will prosper in an increasingly competitive global marketplace.

Reading the Future

One of the standard systems for classifying jobs in Canada is the National Occupational Classification (NOC), developed by Human Resources Development Canada for use in identifying occupational skill shortages, projecting skill needs, and in alerting the education system to the changing skill mix. It is also commonly used to examine issues of equity in Canada's labour markets. As illustrated below, occupations in the NOC are grouped along two dimensions by similarity of skills required.

National occupational classification matrix

Skill type / Skill level	Business, finance and administration occupations	Natural and applied sciences and related occupations	Health occupations	Occupations in social science, education, government service and religion	Occupations in art, culture, recreation and sport	Sales and service occupations	Trades, transport and equipment operators and related occupations	Occupations unique to primary industry	Occupations unique to processing, manufacturing and utilities
Senior management									
Management occupations	Managers	Managers	Managers	Managers	Managers	Managers	Managers	Managers	Managers
Skill Level A	Professional occupations in business and finance	Professional occupations in natural and applied sciences	Professional occupations in health	Professional occupations in social science, education, government services and religion	Professional occupations in art and culture				
Skill Level B	Skilled administrative and business occupations	Technical occupations related to natural and applied sciences	Technical and skilled occupations in health	Paraprofessional occupations in law, social services, education and religion	Technical and skilled occupations in art, culture, recreation and sport	Skilled sales and service occupations	Trades and skilled transport and equipment operators	Skilled occupations in primary industry	Processing, manufacturing and utilities supervisors and skilled operators
Skill Level C	Clerical occupations		Assisting occupations in support of health services			Intermediate sales and service occupations	Intermediate occupations in transport, equipment operation, installation and maintenance	Intermediate occupations in primary industry	Processing and manufacturing machine operators and assemblers
Skill Level D						Elemental sales and service occupations	Trades helpers, construction labourers and related occupations	Labourers in primary industry	Labourers in processing, manufacturing and utilities

Source: Human Resources Development Canada.

The vertical dimension of the NOC classifies occupations into four skill levels[1] based primarily on educational attainment. Occupations at the highest level, Level A, typically require university degrees, while those at Level D, the lowest, typically have no specific educational requirement. This vertical dimension might be thought to reflect levels of generic skill. The horizontal dimension reflects job-specific skills, and is typically associated with different industries. Because literacy is a generic skill, the vertical dimension is more relevant to this report. Table 2.1 reports the literacy skills associated with the major occupational groups, together with the NOC levels typical of the majority of occupations in each group.

---

1. Managerial occupations are an exception to the skill level principle; these occupations are not distinguished by skill, but are grouped into a single level.

Statistics Canada – Catalogue no. 89-551-XPE

Table 2.1

Distribution of literacy by occupation across the three scales, Canadian adults aged 16 and over

Occupation	National Occupational Classification level	Prose scale Level			
		1	2	3	4/5
		%			
Officials/Managers	None	...	23	42	28
Professionals	A	...	15	34	50
Technicians	B	...	26	27	43
Clerical workers	B/C	6	29	51	15
Service/Sales workers	B/C/D	11	29	35	25
Skilled agricultural workers		18	32	37	...
Skilled craft workers	C	30	24	33	14
Machine operators	C	28	22	39	11

Occupation	National Occupational Classification level	Document scale Level			
		1	2	3	4/5
		%			
Officials/Managers	None	...	25	30	40
Professionals	A	...	10	33	55
Technicians	B	...	13	58	26
Clerical workers	B/C	8	27	37	28
Service/Sales workers	B/C/D	16	30	29	25
Skilled agricultural workers		15	36	25	24
Skilled craft workers	C	25	31	29	16
Machine operators	C	27	31	27	15

Occupation	National Occupational Classification level	Quantitative scale Level			
		1	2	3	4/5
		%			
Officials/Managers	None	...	23	35	38
Professionals	A	...	11	37	50
Technicians	B	...	18	34	45
Clerical workers	B/C	...	34	41	19
Service/Sales workers	B/C/D	15	31	41	13
Skilled agricultural workers		19	27	33	21
Skilled craft workers	C	22	35	29	14
Machine operators	C	29	29	33	9

...   Sample size too small to produce reliable estimates.

Some occupations have quite different distributions on different scales. For example, 45% of technicians are at Level 4/5 on the quantitative scale, but only 26% are at this level on the document scale. More clerical workers (28%) are at Level 4/5 on the document scale, than on the prose (15%) and quantitative scales (19%).

Occupations primarily at NOC Levels A (professional) and B (technical, paraprofessional and skilled) are ones in which a significant proportion of the incumbents were at Level 4/5, especially on the prose and quantitative scales. This was particularly true of professional occupations where 50% or more were at the highest level. In these occupations less than 10% were at Level 1.[2]

---

2.   In order to support international comparisons, the occupation and industry data in the IALS were coded to the International Standard Classification of Occupation (ISCO-88) and the International Standard Industrial Classification (ISIC). At the aggregate level presented in this report, these classifications are broadly comparable to the NOC. Appendix C provides breakdowns of each major international occupation.

The IALS findings related to occupation make it clear that it would be quite inappropriate to set a single standard of literacy for Canada. Clerical workers appear to be "literate" at Level 3 while professionals are "literate" at Level 4/5. Higher skill levels may provide many avenues for personal and economic growth, but satisfying and economically rewarding lives can be lived even if one's literacy skill is not at Level 4/5.

Canadian skilled craft workers and machine operators, an occupation seen by many as crucial to sustaining high-wage manufacturing jobs, do slightly better than similar workers in the United States. If Levels 2 and 3 are the critical literacy levels for high-skill manufacturing, then Canada and the United States may not be as well prepared as some of our European competitors.

The IALS data contain some indication that the occupations of the future will be those requiring higher generic skills: occupations that are increasing in number have high literacy scores; those that are declining have relatively low literacy scores.

For occupations at NOC Levels C and D, the proportion at Level 4/5 was smaller and that at Level 1 larger. For example, less than 20% of skilled craft workers and machine operators were at Level 4/5 and nearly one-quarter were at Level 1.

The distribution of literacy skills among clerical workers is particularly interesting. This set of occupations represents almost one-fifth (18.6% in 1991) of the Canadian labour force, about 2.5 million workers, so the literacy consequences of this occupation have large economic impacts. And this is, after all, an occupation that by definition is involved with literacy: clerical workers process documents. Yet the proportion of clerical workers at Level 4/5 was quite small (under 20%), except on the document scale (the scale that represents the kind of text with which clerical workers most often deal) where the proportion at Level 4/5 was close to the proportion of technicians at this level. It appears that clerical workers do not routinely engage in the kind of text synthesis and integration that Level 4/5 requires. And only a small number of clerical workers (less than 10%) were at Level 1, suggesting that although the highest level of skill is not required, clerical work does require mid-level literacy skills.

The IALS findings related to occupation make it clear that it would be quite inappropriate to set a single standard of literacy for Canada. For example, clerical workers appear to be "literate" at Level 3 while professionals are "literate" at Level 4/5. This is not to say that everyone should not aspire to higher skill levels because that clearly provides many avenues for personal and economic growth, but it does mean that satisfying and economically rewarding lives can be lived even if one's literacy skill is not at Level 4/5.

The occupations in which Canada differed most noticeably from other IALS countries were skilled craft workers and machine operators (Table 2.2). The skills of workers in these occupations are seen by many as crucial to sustaining high-wage manufacturing jobs; only if the skills are high can enough value be added to compete with low-wage, low-skill jobs elsewhere. The proportions at Level 4/5 were similar for Canada, Germany and the Netherlands, but the proportions were small, as in clerical occupations, suggesting that here, too, Level 4/5 is not the most significant level. However, two to three times as many Canadian workers in these occupations were at Level 1, and there were 10% to 15% more at Level 3 in these other two countries than in Canada. On the other hand, Canadians fared slightly better than skilled craft workers in the United States. If Levels 2 and 3 are the critical literacy levels for high-skill manufacturing, then Canada and the United States may not be as well prepared as their European competitors. The lower literacy levels in Canada reflect differences in how Canadian firms organize their production processes and the nature of the Canadian labour market.

In the next chapter, the data show that Canadians in these occupations read less on the job than do similar workers in Germany and the Netherlands. If jobs are not designed to promote literacy skill by asking workers to use their skills, then the workers will inevitably end up with lower levels of literacy.

It is widely reported that the occupations of the future will be those requiring higher generic skills. The IALS data contain some indication to support these claims. Figure 2.1 shows the relation between changes in the proportion of Canadian workers in an occupation and the average prose literacy score of workers in that occupation. The occupations appear to form two common clusters on the two axes: those occupations that were increasing and in which the literacy scores were relatively high, and those that were decreasing and in which the literacy scores were relatively low. The relationship between literacy and occupational change is not exact because the occupation with the greatest growth, managers, did not have the highest average literacy scores. The general trend, however, is strong.

Table 2.2

Comparison of the distribution of document reading literacy for skilled craft workers and machine operators in the IALS countries, adults aged 16 to 65

Skilled craft workers and machine operators in	Document scale Level			
	1	2	3	4/5
	%			
Canada	25	31	29	16
Germany	7	33	47	14
Netherlands	9	36	39	16
Poland	47	30	17	6
Sweden	8	17	45	30
Switzerland (French)	22	29	32	17
Switzerland (German)	22	37	33	9
United States	30	38	25	7

There are similar proportions at Level 4/5 in Canada, Germany and the Netherlands, but Canada has many more skilled craft workers and machine operators at Level 1 than either of these countries.

Figure 2.1

The relation between changes in employment and average prose literacy skill, by occupation in Canada, adults aged 16 and over in the labour force

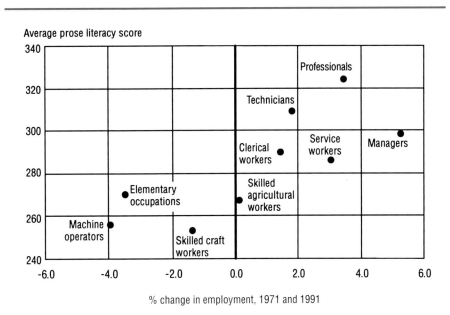

% change in employment, 1971 and 1991

The occupations that have grown in the past 20 years have higher average literacy scores than the occupations that have declined. It is interesting though, that the two occupations with the highest growth, managers and service workers, are not the ones with the highest literacy scores. In particular, service occupations have the lowest scores of the growth occupations, although the average is still higher than that of any declining occupation.

The IALS also shows a strong relationship between industrial growth and skill. The industries that have experienced growth are the ones whose employees have relatively high levels of skill; those that are declining are characterized by lower skills.

Literacy and industry

The trend demonstrated in Figure 2.1 is not unique to Canada. In all the IALS countries, employment growth areas are high literacy areas. The most useful international data on employment changes, the OECD Jobs Study (OECD 1994), is based on industry rather than occupational change. When paired with this data, the IALS also shows a strong relationship between growth and skill (Figure 2.2). The industries that have experienced growth are the ones whose employees have relatively high levels of skill; those that are declining are characterized by lower skills. The exception in Canada is agriculture; while this industry is not among the more highly skilled, the skill level is high relative to other low-growth industries, particularly when compared with the same sector in Germany.

Figure 2.2

The relation between changes in employment and average prose literacy skill, by industry in Germany and Canada, adults aged 16 to 65

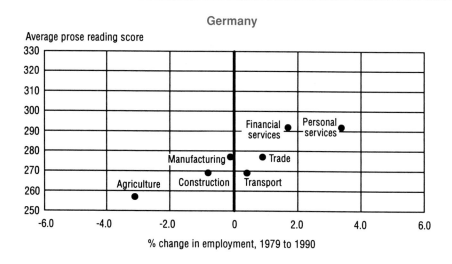

Germany

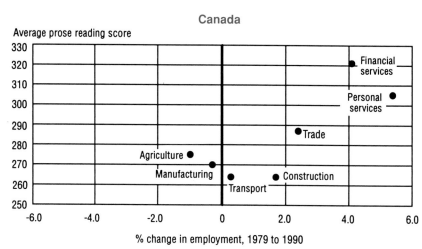

Canada

Industries where there has been growth are industries where the employees have high literacy skills. On the other hand, employees in those industries that have decreased tend to have relatively low skills.

Financial services and personal services have the most highly skilled work force despite having a similar age profile to other industries.

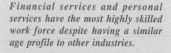

The distribution of skills by industry (Table 2.3) is generally less revealing than that by occupation, because most industries employ a variety of occupations; clerical workers, for example, work in most industries.[3] Nonetheless, there are some interesting relationships between skill and industry. As the growth patterns in Figure 2.2 suggest, financial services and personal services have the most highly skilled work force. Fewer than 10% were at Level 1, regardless of scale. On each scale, the two industries with the largest proportions at Level 4/5 were financial services and personal services. It is notable, though, that to the extent the data in Table 2.3 reflect a supply–demand factor, financial services are considerably less demanding of prose skills than of document and quantitative skills.

---

3. The distribution of industries, and occupations for that matter, at this level of aggregation shows little variation from region to region in Canada. Consequently, regional differences in industry and occupation cannot be captured at the level of analysis the IALS sample permits. Thus, it is not possible to estimate how much differences in occupation and industry contribute to the regional distribution of literacy in Canada.

Statistics Canada – Catalogue no. 89-551-XPE

Table 2.3

Distribution of literacy by industry across the three scales, Canadian adults aged 16 and over

	Prose scale Level			
Industry	1	2	3	4/5
	%			
Agriculture	20	28	39	...
Manufacturing	24	19	42	15
Construction	28	26	29	...
Trade	12	31	37	20
Transport	...	29	33	22
Financial services	...	26	47	25
Personal services	7	21	33	39

	Document scale Level			
Industry	1	2	3	4/5
	%			
Agriculture	18	35	28	19
Manufacturing	21	24	32	23
Construction	27	33	29	...
Trade	14	29	32	25
Transport	...	28	32	27
Financial services	...	16	34	47
Personal services	8	20	40	32

	Quantitative scale Level			
Industry	1	2	3	4/5
	%			
Agriculture	21	29	31	19
Manufacturing	21	29	29	21
Construction	26	29	32	...
Trade	13	34	38	16
Transport	...	20	36	25
Financial services	...	20	36	43
Personal services	8	20	40	33

... Sample size too small to produce reliable estimates.

Across the scales, of all industries, financial and personal services have the largest proportions at Level 4/5 and the smallest at Level 1.

It might be thought that both financial services and personal services have higher skills because they have younger work forces than other industries, and thus are simply capitalizing on the fact that younger adults (those entering service sector jobs) have higher literacy skills than older Canadians (those whose manufacturing jobs are being threatened). However, the age profiles of the industries are quite similar. The average age of workers in the financial services industry in the IALS data is 37.7; the average of the IALS respondents in manufacturing is 37.8. The industry with the youngest average age is trade,[4] with a mean age of 32.0. Personal services has an even older average age, 39.0, than finance or manufacturing.

Traditionally, industry, occupation and educational attainment have been assumed to be uniform, and thus reliable predictors of skill: a clerk is a clerk, a secondary school graduate is a secondary school graduate. The wide variation in skill revealed in these groups by the IALS raises serious concerns about their use by employers as screening devices for access to employment, and supports a shift to objective skill testing in both schools and the workplace.

Traditionally, industry, occupation and educational attainment have been assumed to be uniform, and thus reliable predictors of skill: a clerical worker is a clerical worker, a secondary school graduate is a secondary school graduate. The wide variation in skill revealed in these groups by the IALS raises serious concerns about the use of these "proxy" variables by employers as screening devices for access to employment, and supports a shift to objective skill testing in both schools and the workplace.

4. Most occupations in trade are service jobs.

Literacy and employment

The majority of adults read mostly at work; in this, Canada is no different than other countries. Therefore, individuals who are unemployed are less likely to read than those who are at work or in school. This lack of reading practice is a problem for many unemployed people because their literacy skills are already relatively low (Table 2.4).

Table 2.4

Distribution of literacy by employment status across the three scales, Canadian adults aged 16 and over

| | Prose scale | | | |
| | Level | | | |
Current employment status	1	2	3	4/5
		%		
Employed	12	25	37	26
Unemployed	33	23	36	9
Student	12	23	40	26
Retired	49	28	19	5
Homemaker	27	28	28	18
Other, out of labour force[1]	43	35	19	...

| | Document scale | | | |
| | Level | | | |
Current employment status	1	2	3	4/5
		%		
Employed	12	24	35	29
Unemployed	30	29	23	17
Student	8	26	32	34
Retired	55	22	18	5
Homemaker	36	24	32	9
Other, out of labour force[1]	51	29	15	...

| | Quantitative scale | | | |
| | Level | | | |
Current employment status	1	2	3	4/5
		%		
Employed	11	25	36	27
Unemployed	33	31	27	9
Student	8	27	45	21
Retired	49	27	18	6
Homemaker	31	25	33	11
Other, out of labour force[1]	47	29	19	...

1. According to Statistics Canada's definition, the employed are persons having a job or business, whereas the unemployed are without work, available for work, and actively seeking work. Together the unemployed and employed constitute the labour force.

... Sample size too small to produce reliable estimates.

About three times as many unemployed Canadians are at Level 1, compared with those who are employed. The skills of those who are still students are largely comparable with those of the employed population, but because they have not yet completed their education they will likely enter the labour force with generally higher skills.

Someone who is unemployed is about three times as likely to be at Level 1 as someone who is employed. And, except on the document scale, an employed person is three times as likely to be at Level 4/5 as someone who is unemployed.

Someone who was unemployed was about three times as likely to be at Level 1 as someone who was employed (32% to 33% of the unemployed were at Level 1 regardless of scale, compared with 12% of the employed). And, except on the document scale, an employed person was three times as likely to be at Level 4/5 as someone who was unemployed. Considered from the other perspective (Table 2.5), 24% of those at Level 1 on the document scale were in the work force but were unemployed, and only 7% of those at Level 4/5 on this scale were in the labour force and without work.[5] Quantitative and prose literacy show even larger effects on unemployment, with 26% of those at Level 1 on these scales unemployed, compared with only 4% of those at Level 4/5.

---

5. According to Statistics Canada's definition, the employed are persons having a job or business, whereas the unemployed are without work, available for work, and actively seeking work. Together the unemployed and employed constitute the labour force.

Table 2.5

The distribution of employment status by literacy level for all three scales, Canadian adults aged 16 and over in the labour force

	Current employment status	
Prose scale	Employed	Unemployed
	%	
Level 1	74	26
Level 2	90	10
Level 3	90	10
Level 4/5	96	4

	Current employment status	
Document scale	Employed	Unemployed
	%	
Level 1	76	24
Level 2	87	13
Level 3	93	8
Level 4/5	93	7

	Current employment status	
Quantitative scale	Employed	Unemployed
	%	
Level 1	74	26
Level 2	87	13
Level 3	92	8
Level 4/5	96	4

About one-quarter of those in Level 1 who are in the labour force (working or looking for work) are unemployed. The higher the literacy level, the less likely someone is to be unemployed.

Individuals with higher skills work more weeks each year when they do work. The differences between Level 1 and Level 4/5 represent about a month's difference in work over the course of a year.

Further, individuals with higher skills worked more weeks each year when they did work (Table 2.6). There is a statistically significant relationship between literacy skill and weeks worked. In particular, those at Level 1 were likely to work fewer weeks than those at any other level, and those at Level 2 were more likely to work fewer weeks than those at Level 4/5. However, the differences between Levels 2 and 3 and the differences between Levels 3 and 4/5 are not significant. The differences between Level 1 and Level 4/5 represent about a month's difference in work over the course of a year.

Table 2.6

The average number of weeks worked by literacy level for the three scales, Canadian adults aged 16 and over who worked in the previous year

	Average number of weeks worked
Prose scale	
Level 1	39.5
Level 2	43.6
Level 3	43.3
Level 4/5	45.0
Document scale	
Level 1	37.5
Level 2	43.1
Level 3	44.3
Level 4/5	45.0
Quantitative scale	
Level 1	38.4
Level 2	42.6
Level 3	44.4
Level 4/5	44.9

Individuals at higher literacy levels were more likely to be employed.

Again, it is important to stress that the association between employment and literacy set out here should not be interpreted as differences in literacy skill leading to differences in employment. Because literacy skills are most often used in the workplace, it may be the inability to find regular employment, and the opportunity to use and enhance literacy skill that follows from it, that plays a role in low skill.

Literacy and social transfers

Because Canada has relatively high levels of employee turnover, many individuals are unemployed for relatively short periods of time, particularly when compared with unemployed workers in European countries where the labour market is more rigid. Canadian employment policy has long focused on bringing the long-term unemployed into the labour force, although recent evaluations have suggested that the traditional programs have not always been successful.[6] The IALS has no simple measure of "long-term unemployment," but it is likely that individuals who receive some form of social assistance other than Unemployment Insurance (UI)[7] have been out of the labour force for some time.

Canadians who experience a loss of paid employment or are unable to find sufficient employment may receive income support from government programs. Those who have been in the labour force are eligible for Unemployment Insurance if they have worked sufficient qualifying weeks and if they have not been unemployed longer than the specified eligibility period.[8] Others who are unemployed are eligible for social assistance; some who receive UI may also receive social assistance if their UI payments fall below the social assistance standard. A key question for policy makers is the degree to which a lack of skills in these populations might constitute a barrier to increased participation in the labour force. Table 2.7 displays the distribution of various categories of income support by literacy level for adults in the traditional working-age group, 16 to 65.

---

6. See, for example, "The impact of CETA programmes on earnings: A review of the literature," *Journal of Human Resources*, B. Barnow 1987; "Evaluation of labour market policy in Sweden," *Evaluating Labour Market and Social Programmes: The State of a Complex Art*, A. Björklund 1991; "The estimation of wage gains and welfare gains in self-selection models," *The Review of Economics and Statistics*, A. Björklund and R. Moffitt 1987; "Incentive effects of the US welfare system: A review," *Journal of Economic Literature*, R. Moffitt 1992; "Evaluation of manpower and training programmes: The North American experience," *Evaluating Labour Market and Social Programmes: The State of a Complex Art*, C. Riddell 1991; "An event history approach to the evaluation of training, recruitment and employment programmes," *Journal of Applied Econometrics*, G. Ridder 1986.

7. The federal Unemployment Insurance program has been redesigned and its name changed to Employment Insurance; at the time of the IALS survey (1994), the program was known as Unemployment Insurance.

8. The number of weeks needed to qualify varies across the country depending on the unemployment rate in the region. A large number of UI recipients are employed in industries that operate only on a seasonal, part-year basis.

Table 2.7

The distribution of literacy by income support category, Canadian adults aged 16 to 65

| | Prose scale | | | |
| | Level | | | |
Income support	1	2	3	4/5
		%		
Unemployment Insurance	19	30	37	14
Social assistance recipient	37	28	27	9
None	14	24	36	27
	Document scale			
	Level			
Income support	1	2	3	4/5
		%		
Unemployment Insurance	22	31	27	21
Social assistance recipient	42	25	24	9
None	14	23	34	28
	Quantitative scale			
	Level			
Income support	1	2	3	4/5
		%		
Unemployment Insurance	18	30	33	18
Social assistance recipient	42	28	24	7
None	14	25	37	25

Those receiving no support are more likely to be at higher levels than those receiving Unemployment Insurance, who are in turn less likely to be at lower levels than general social assistance recipients (SAR). The SAR group has significantly lower education than the other two groups, but there are only minor differences in education between those who receive UI and those who do not receive any income support. Those in the UI group, however, are more likely to have worked in occupations and industries with lower literacy demands and practices.

The social assistance recipients (SAR) demonstrate markedly lower literacy skills than either Unemployment Insurance beneficiaries or the general population, with over one-third at Level 1 (compared with 22% of the adult population) and less than 10% at Level 4/5 (compared with 20% of the population as a whole). Those receiving UI benefits tended to have higher skills than those in the SAR group but not as high as those who received no benefits from either of these programs. On all scales, those who did not receive income support have larger proportions at higher levels than either of the income support groups.

Differences in educational attainment play a large role in understanding the lower scores of the SARs; 60% of this group did not complete secondary school, compared with 29% of those receiving no benefits and 28% of the UI recipients.[9] However, there were no large differences between the other two groups, although 23% of the UI group completed secondary school. The lower scores of the UI group may be related to their less frequent literacy practices, itself a consequence of their less frequent attachment to the work force and to the fact that their employment is more likely to be in occupations with lower literacy demands. Nonetheless, UI recipients were more like those receiving neither UI nor social assistance than were SARs because most had worked recently (otherwise they would not qualify for UI). Many UI recipients are seasonally unemployed or only temporarily out of a job as part of the turnover that characterizes the Canadian labour market.

9. A discussion of the reasons for such differences is beyond the scope of this report, but studies would suggest that low literacy skills may lead to poor school performance leading, in turn, to early departure. See, for example, *Literacy and Poverty - A View from the Inside*, National Anti-Poverty Organization 1993.

The IALS Canadian data offer ample evidence that literacy programs designed for individuals receiving income support would meet a significant need. If employment growth continues to be concentrated in those occupations and industries with high skill demands, income support recipients are likely to find it increasingly difficult to enter or re-enter the labour force unless afforded with the opportunity to develop their literacy skills.

Literacy and adult education and training

The IALS data show that adult education and training programs are less likely to reach those with low skills because much of the adult education and training goes to those who are already highly skilled. In this, the IALS data are consistent with other Statistics Canada studies of adult education and training.[10]

General training and upgrading have concerned government policy makers for some time. In a society that appears to want to embrace lifelong learning, significant numbers of citizens may be excluded due to low literacy skills—skills that might restrict their ability to participate in adult education and training. There is widespread belief that training is important to a country's economic success and that of its individual citizens. At the same time, there is concern that adult education and training work to increase inequality because it mostly serves to increase the skills of the already skilled.[11] The concern is not exclusively Canadian, however; the IALS data show that in all participating countries more individuals at high skill levels had received adult education and training in the last year than those individuals at low skill levels (Table 2.8). Because the international comparisons include only 16- to 65-year-olds, Table 2.9 includes the same information for the complete Canadian sample, although no new relationships occur. A more complete analysis is expected in a UNESCO comparative study of the IALS adult education and training data.[12]

Table 2.8

Proportion of each literacy level, prose scale, who have participated in adult education or training in the last year, adults aged 16 to 65

	Prose scale Level			
	1	2	3	4/5
		%		
Canada	21	34	50	58
Germany	8	15	19	34
Netherlands	23	32	46	58
Poland	9	16	23	42
Sweden	29	41	52	60
Switzerland (French)	20	29	43	57
Switzerland (German)	23	39	57	72
United States	18	34	51	66

10. *Adult Education and Training Survey*, Statistics Canada 1992.

11. The evidence regarding the efficacy of adult training is mixed but seems to favour early interventions. See, for example, *Evidence on the Effectiveness of Youth Labour Market Programs in Canada: An Assessment*, W. Craig Riddell 1996.

12. *The Emergence of Learning Societies: Who Participates in Adult Learning*, UNESCO (in press).

Table 2.9

Proportion of adults who participated in adult education and training, by level, prose scale, for the full Canadian sample aged 16 and over

Prose scale	Participation in adult education and training % who participated
Level 1	14
Level 2	31
Level 3	48
Level 4/5	57

Slightly smaller proportions of the full sample reported participation compared with Table 2.8 because this table (Table 2.9) includes older Canadians who have lower participation.

A remarkably low proportion of retired adults and of those over 65 participated in adult education.

Other characteristics related to the incidence of adult education and training are reported in Table 2.10. Of particular note is the low proportion of retired adults and of those over 65 (much the same group, of course) who participated in adult education and training. Despite the growth of educational programs directed towards older adults, the low numbers here are striking;[13] participation appears to decline in all older age groups. While it might seem that the large proportion of 16- to 25-year-olds who received adult education and training would naturally reflect the fact that many were still in school, it also reflects the fact that much of the reported adult education and training is given to new workers, who are more likely to be 16 to 25. Table 2.10 contains participation rates by age for those who were employed at the time of the IALS. This group reflects the overall pattern by age.

Table 2.10

Proportion of adults who participated in adult education and training, by various characteristics, Canadian adults aged 16 and over

	Participation in adult education and training % who participated
Current employment status	
Employed	45
Unemployed	32
Homemaker	22
Retired	8
Age group	
16 to 25	71
26 to 35	42
36 to 45	42
46 to 55	33
56 to 65	15
Over 65	8
Age group, employed	
16 to 25	61
26 to 35	44
36 to 45	43
46 to 55	39
56 to 65	31
Over 65	...
Men	40
Women	37

...   Sample size too small to produce reliable estimates.

More young adults receive training, both because many are still in school and because much of the workplace training is focused on new workers, who are typically young adults. The low proportion of adults over 65 who participate is a result of the decline in participation upon retirement because much adult education is organized by and through the workplace.

---

13. It is possible that older adults do not regard the courses they take as training or education, so this may underestimate the actual incidence. The questions used in the IALS were taken from the Adult Education and Training Survey (Statistics Canada 1992). The phrasing of these questions had been carefully researched, but primarily with adults in the typical working years.

It might be thought that the participation rate is higher for those at higher skill levels because the courses that would be attractive to individuals with lower skills are not available. However, more individuals at higher levels reported the courses they wanted were unavailable, whether the course was for work or for interest (Table 2.11). These findings suggest that literacy policy should address the needs of those who might benefit from adult education and training but who do not now participate and who do not identify needs that might be served by training and education.

Table 2.11

Proportion of adults at each literacy level, prose scale, who reported that there was some education or training they wanted but were unable to get, both for work and for personal interest, Canadian adults aged 16 and over

	Is there training or education you wanted, but could not take?	
Prose scale	Yes: Personal interest	Yes: Work-related
	%	
Level 1	13	11
Level 2	25	22
Level 3	32	30
Level 4/5	40	35

Not only do more individuals at higher levels receive training (Table 2.9), but they would take more if possible. Why individuals at lower levels are less interested in training and education requires further research.

Literacy and part-time work

Some elements of employment are independent of literacy skill. There has been considerable concern about growth in part-time employment relative to full-time work. The data suggest that differences in skill may have little role in whether work is full- or part-time (Table 2.12). Individuals work part time for a number of reasons. Table 2.12 distinguishes three types of part-time workers: those who would prefer full-time work if it were available; those who work part time because they are still in school; and those who prefer to work part time (voluntary part-time workers). As the students tend to be slightly more educated as a group (most are postsecondary students), the proportions of this group at Levels 1 and 2 are low. Those who want full-time work do not differ greatly from those already working full time, though there are notably fewer of them at Level 4/5 on the quantitative scale. Those working part time voluntarily also look much like the full-time workers, though there are slightly more of them at higher levels. The majority of the part-time workers other than students are female: 71% of those who would rather work full time and 86% of those who voluntarily work part time are women. Because women tend to score higher on the prose scale and slightly lower on the document and quantitative scales, the differences between full-time and non-student part-time literacy may simply be the difference between male (full-time) and female (part-time) patterns.

Table 2.12

The distribution of literacy by type of employment, Canadian adults aged 16 and over in the labour force

| | Prose scale | | | |
| | | Level | | |
Type of work in most recent job	1	2	3	4/5
		%		
Full time	14	26	36	24
Part time (wanted full time)	15	17	42	26
Part time (student)	3	16	49	32
Part time (other)	...	22	33	36

| | Document scale | | | |
| | | Level | | |
Type of work in most recent job	1	2	3	4/5
		%		
Full time	14	24	34	27
Part time (wanted full time)	9	25	42	23
Part time (student)	2	14	37	47
Part time (other)	...	29	28	32

| | Quantitative scale | | | |
| | | Level | | |
Type of work in most recent job	1	2	3	4/5
		%		
Full time	13	26	35	27
Part time (wanted full time)	15	27	41	16
Part time (student)	4	20	56	21
Part time (other)	...	28	30	30

...   Sample size too small to produce reliable estimates.

Except on the quantitative scale, there is little difference between individuals who work full time and those who work part time. This suggests that literacy skill plays little role in determining whether someone finds full- or part-time work.

Literacy and income

Income is one aspect of employment where it may be reasonable to draw a causal association. If employers pay workers for their skill, as rational economics would predict, then individuals with low skill ought to receive lower incomes than those with higher skill. Table 2.13 presents the distribution of literacy by income for those in the IALS sample who worked in the previous year; the pattern suggests a relationship between literacy and wage/salary income. The effect is not uniform across skill. The proportion of those at Levels 1, 2 and 3 who are in the lowest income quintile is about the same, though the proportion of those with high skill, Level 4/5, in the lowest quintile is considerably smaller. However, when the whole picture is considered, it is apparent there is a major income penalty for having low skill. Approximately 71% of those at Level 1 on the quantitative scale had incomes below the middle quintile, Quintile 3, but only about 58% of those at Level 2 had incomes this low. Less than 50% of those at Level 3, and even less, about 35% of those in Level 4/5, were in the bottom half of the distribution.

Table 2.13

Distribution of levels of income from wages and salary by literacy levels, Canadian adults aged 16 and over reporting wage income

| | Prose scale | | | | |
| | Income quintile[1] | | | | |
	1	2	3	4	5
			%		
Level 1	26	34	21	13	...
Level 2	23	20	18	24	16
Level 3	23	19	19	19	21
Level 4/5	18	15	18	20	29

| | Document scale | | | | |
| | Income quintile[1] | | | | |
	1	2	3	4	5
			%		
Level 1	25	39	15	10	...
Level 2	25	19	21	18	17
Level 3	21	17	23	23	16
Level 4/5	20	15	14	22	30

| | Quantitative scale | | | | |
| | Income quintile[1] | | | | |
	1	2	3	4	5
			%		
Level 1	28	31	25	9	...
Level 2	23	24	22	14	17
Level 3	25	18	13	26	17
Level 4/5	13	13	21	22	32

1. Income quintile ranges: 1 = $1 to $8,000; 2 = $8,001 to $18,000; 3 = $18,001 to $27,000; 4 = $27,001 to $40,000; 5 = $40,001 and over.

... Sample size too small to produce reliable estimates.

Individuals with low literacy skills are much less likely to have high income than are individuals with high literacy skills. Quantitative literacy appears to have a larger impact ($r^2 = .23$) than prose ($r^2 = .17$) or document ($r^2 = .16$) literacy.

The relationship between income and literacy is weaker for those in Levels 2 and 3. While those in Level 3 are somewhat more likely to be in Quintile 5, similar proportions of both levels are above Quintile 3 on the prose and document scales. On the quantitative scale, individuals at Level 3 are more likely to be above Quintile 3 (45%) than are those at Level 2 (31%). In general, quantitative literacy has a larger impact on income than do prose or document literacy. Quantitative literacy is generally more influential on employment characteristics than the other two types of literacy skills.

Economists have traditionally looked upon North American labour markets as flexible compared with those in Europe. It might be expected, then, that skill would play a larger role in income in North America than in Europe. The IALS data offer an opportunity to examine the differential effect of literacy in several economies. Figure 2.3 presents comparative data for the two North American economies in the IALS, Canada and the United States, and two European economies, Germany and the Netherlands.[14] The figure shows, for example, that in Canada, of Level 1 individuals, 20% less are at Quintile 3 and above compared with Level 3. Notably, Levels 1 and 4/5 differ more from Level 3 in Canada and the United States than they do in Germany and the Netherlands. In fact, in the former, there is only a small difference, approximately 10 percentage points, between the proportion of those at Level 1 with Quintile 3 and above incomes and the proportion of those at Level 3 with this income. There is a slightly larger "penalty" in the Netherlands for being at Level 1, but the "bonus" for being at

14. Sweden is excluded because the small numbers in lower literacy levels (see Table 2.2) make comparisons difficult; Switzerland is excluded because of some problems in coding low levels of income.

Level 4/5 is about the same as in Germany: less than 10%. In Canada and the United States, however, there is a relatively large bonus for being at Level 4/5. Although the differences between the two North American countries are small, the data do suggest that income is slightly more sensitive to skill in the United States than it is in Canada, fitting with the conventional analysis that sees Canada as having a slightly more rigid labour market than the United States.[15]

Figure 2.3

The effect of literacy skill on income in four countries, adults aged 16 to 65

The bars represent the proportion at each literacy level whose income is in Quintile 3 and above relative to the proportion of literacy Level 3 whose income is in the upper three quintiles. Literacy has only a small effect on income in Germany and a relatively small effect in the Netherlands compared with Canada and the United States.

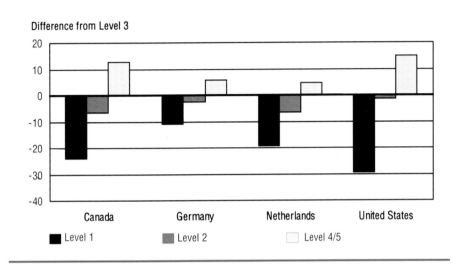

Difference from Level 3

| Canada | Germany | Netherlands | United States |

■ Level 1   ▨ Level 2   ☐ Level 4/5

The IALS reveals a strong association between income and literacy, with quantitative literacy having the largest impact. In Canada and the United States, however, both the income penalty for having low skills and the income bonus for high skills are larger than in those observed in the Netherlands or Germany. A broader awareness of the size of these income differentials might allow more Canadians to make informed choices about participation in remedial literacy education.

The IALS reveals a strong association between income and literacy, with quantitative literacy having the largest impact. In Canada and the United States, however, both the income penalty for having low skills and the income bonus for high skills are larger than those observed in the Netherlands or Germany. A broader awareness of the size of these income differentials might allow more Canadians to make informed choices about participation in remedial literacy education.

Clearly literacy has consequences. The comparative data from the IALS suggest that government policies have an influence on how those consequences work themselves out in a particular country. Canada's immigration policy has brought significant numbers of highly skilled immigrants to the country; no other IALS country has a similar pattern of literacy among immigrants. Chapters 1 and 2 of this report have clearly demonstrated that income, education, labour market and immigration policies affect the distribution of literacy skills in the adult population. We have also seen that individuals can have a profound impact on their own literacy skill: fully 10% of adults tested demonstrated literacy levels well beyond what their formal education would indicate.

Throughout, the analysis has suggested that literacy practices play an important role in maintaining and enhancing literacy skill. It has further been suggested that jobs may cause literacy as much as they require it because a great deal of the reading that Canadian adults do is done at work. If a job dictates that little reading needs to be done, little use of the skill will take place. What remains is to fill in the picture of the connections between work, daily life, reading practices and skill: that is the role of the next chapter.

---

15. For a series of studies on labour market flexibility see *Working under different rules*, Richard B. Freeman, ed., 1994.

Chapter 3

Literacy practices in Canada

Stan Jones
Consultant in Adult Literacy and Adult Education

L iteracy skills matter, of course, because people need to read, write, and calculate at work and in their daily lives. In turn, the daily use of skills has the power to sustain and enhance those skills. Thus there is considerable importance in describing the way in which literacy and literacy activities are part of our lives. As part of the IALS interview, respondents were asked about a broad range of literacy activities, both at work and at home, and about other activities that, if not directly related to literacy, impinge on literacy.[1] The patterns across all reading and literacy activities are similar: individuals with higher literacy skills engage in literacy-related activities more frequently and in greater depth. This chapter describes these practices and their relation to other individual characteristics. The findings will interest those whose concerns are the match between curricula and the skill needs demanded by the labour market, particularly at the entry level.

Different occupations impose different literacy demands. By the nature of the job itself, clerical workers would, for example, be expected to use some types of literacy more frequently than machine operators and vice versa.

Literacy and the three Rs at work

Table 3.1 sets out the relationship between various occupations and typical reading tasks.

Table 3.1

Proportion of workers in major occupational groupings who reported engaging in various workplace reading tasks at least once a week, Canadian adults aged 16 and over in the labour force

Occupation	Do you read . . . at least once a week?				
	letters or memos	reports, articles, magazines or journals	manuals or reference books, including catalogues	diagrams or schematics	bills, invoices, spreadsheets or budget tables
			%		
Managers	90	83	84	50	86
Professionals	95	85	81	52	56
Technicians	77	70	48	29	45
Clerical workers	84	53	46	15	52
Service workers	59	42	33	15	45
Skilled craft workers	43	30	37	50	33
Machine operators	58	42	33	33	34
Elementary occupations	46	27	28	28	38

Occupations that typically have higher skill requirements are those in which the workers report higher frequencies for these tasks. However, there are some tasks that are particularly important for certain occupations. Clerical workers, for example, deal with letters and memos more than expected for their general skill level.

---

1. These questions greatly expanded on the questions about literacy practices that were part of the 1989 Survey of Literacy Skills Used in Daily Activities (LSUDA), reflecting the evolution of our understanding of the nature and importance of literacy practices, an importance that was signalled by the analysis of the LSUDA data.

Clearly there are considerable variations in reading practices. While managers and professionals typically report the most frequent use of each type of text, there are marked differences from type to type for other occupations. For example, although clerical workers reported the second most frequent use of letters and memos, they were but seventh in frequency for diagrams and schematics. Of course, one would not expect clerical workers to find themselves confronted with diagrams or schematics very often, though the high frequency for letters would be expected. In most cases, as in the clerical workers' case, the relative frequency makes sense. Skilled craft workers and machine operators need to be able to read diagrams and schematics, but there is much less need for clerical workers and service workers to do so. The data show that 50% of skilled craft workers and 33% of machine operators reported reading diagrams at least once a week, while only 15% of the clerical workers and service workers did so. Some texts, of course, are common to many occupations. For example, workers in all occupations need to be able to read documents about money (bills, invoices and spreadsheets) and manuals. Excluding professionals and managers, whose literacy practices are notably higher than other workers, the least difference among occupations is for manuals and bills, invoices and spreadsheets. Interestingly, while the reading practices reported by professionals are very similar to those for managers on most task types, they were markedly lower for the monetary documents. It is important, therefore, to explore the type of reading that is done and not merely ask about the frequency of reading.

Similar differences exist for writing (Table 3.2), and arithmetic (Table 3.3). Managers and professionals are usually the occupations that do such tasks most frequently, although professionals say they do not fill in bills or invoices as often as do clerical workers; this is consistent with their report of a relatively low frequency of reading such documents. When comparisons are made between reading and writing for similar tasks, it turns out that reading, not unexpectedly, is usually a more common activity than writing. For example, 84% of clerical workers reported reading memos and letters at least once a week, but only 64% reported writing them. However, the writing task is not simply a less frequent mirror image of the reading task. While reading monetary documents is one of the tasks with similar reading frequency across occupations, it is the writing task that most differentiates the occupations other than managers and professionals.

Table 3.2

Proportion of respondents by major occupational groupings who reported engaging in various workplace writing tasks at least once a week, Canadian adults aged 16 and over in the labour force

	Do you write . . . at least once a week?			
Occupation	letters or memos	forms or things such as bills, invoices or budgets	reports or articles	estimates or technical specifications
		%		
Managers	86	85	63	47
Professionals	83	46	67	41
Technicians	49	37	37	24
Clerical workers	64	63	34	14
Service workers	42	47	27	15
Skilled craft workers	33	29	28	36
Machine operators	37	42	38	29
Elementary occupations	34	36	20	16

The arithmetic differences (Table 3.3), appear to be related to traditional distinctions between blue-collar and white-collar jobs. The former (skilled craft workers, machine operators, and those in elementary occupations) report more frequent use of measurement arithmetic, using their skills to determine size and weight. The white-collar workers (clerical workers, service workers) say they do arithmetic (for costs, prices and budgets) more often.

Table 3.3

Proportion of workers in major occupational groupings who reported engaging in each of two workplace numeracy tasks at least once a week, Canadian adults aged 16 and over in the labour force

| | Do you use mathematics at least once a week to . . . | |
| | measure or estimate the size or weight of objects? | calculate prices, costs or budgets? |
Occupation		
	%	
Managers	61	72
Professionals	43	56
Technicians	31	40
Clerical workers	41	52
Service workers	43	58
Skilled craft workers	67	41
Machine operators	56	30
Elementary occupations	48	37

Typical blue-collar workers (skilled craft workers, machine operators, and those in elementary occupations) are more likely to report frequent use of measurement math, while those in traditional white-collar occupations are more likely to report high frequencies of math involving money.

While the data in Tables 3.1 through 3.3 indicate different patterns of literacy depending on the task, they do not directly point to overall, general differences among the occupations. To capture both the variety of different reading tasks and the frequency with which each task is undertaken in a single measure, an index of reading intensity was derived. The reading intensity index has a maximum value of 6, the score for someone who reports doing all six reading tasks probed by the IALS at least once a week. A similar index was created for writing intensity.[2] The writing intensity index has a maximum value of 4, as respondents were only asked about four workplace writing activities (letters or memos; forms or things such as bills, invoices, or budgets; reports or articles; and, estimates or technical specifications). Table 3.4 shows the average reading and writing score on these intensity indices for each of the occupations.

Table 3.4

Average scores and standard deviations for major occupational groupings on a scale of reading and writing intensity (based on the frequency with which individuals carry out tasks and the variety of tasks they carry out), Canadian adults aged 16 and over in the labour force

| | Reading and writing intensity scale | | | |
| | Reading intensity (maximum = 6) | | Writing intensity (maximum = 4) | |
Occupation	Mean	Standard deviation	Mean	Standard deviation
Managers	4.3	1.4	2.8	1.2
Professionals	4.2	1.4	2.4	1.3
Technicians	3.0	1.7	1.5	1.5
Clerical workers	2.7	1.5	1.7	1.1
Service workers	2.3	1.8	1.3	1.3
Skilled craft workers	2.0	2.0	1.3	1.4
Machine operators	2.2	2.0	1.4	1.5
Elementary occupations	1.9	2.0	1.0	1.2

The intensity index represents the range of reading tasks with which an individual must cope. Occupations differ significantly in their averages on this scale.

The standard statistical tests show measurable differences across occupations on both indices.[3] These tests indicate that some differences exist, but they do not indicate that each occupation differs from all the others. Indeed, the results indicate that some pairs of occupations are very similar on the index. A further measure[4] provides insight into the statistically reliable differences in the reading intensity index.

---

2. As there are only two numeracy tasks, an index that combines them would not be appropriate.

3. Reading: $df = 8,3747$, $F = 112.7$, $p < .001$; writing: $df = 8, 3800$, $F = 83.2$, $p < .001$.

4. Newman–Keuls post hoc analysis.

Managers/professionals	Do not differ from each other but have statistically higher reading index scores than all other occupations.
Technicians	Lower reading index scores than managers and professionals, but higher than all others.
Clerical workers	Lower reading index scores than technicians, managers and professionals, but higher than others.
Service workers and machine operators	Lower reading index scores than clerical workers, technicians, managers, and professionals and higher scores than those in elementary occupations, but same scores as each other and as skilled craft workers.
Skilled craft workers	Same reading index scores as service workers, machine operators and elementary occupations, but lower scores than all other occupations.
Elementary occupations	Lower reading index scores than all other occupations except skilled craft workers.

It is worth noting that these differences in reading correspond roughly to the National Occupational Classification (NOC) levels, with the NOC Level A occupations having the highest reading index scores. However, the writing index scores do not fit the NOC model quite as consistently, rendering the NOC levels a less reliable proxy of skill demands in the writing domain.

The post hoc analysis of the writing intensity index shows similarities to the reading intensity index, but there are some notable differences.[5] In particular, technicians report less writing and more reading than clerical workers.

Managers	Have higher writing index scores than any other occupation.
Professionals	Lower writing index scores than managers, but higher than all others.
Clerical workers	Lower writing index scores than managers and professionals, but higher than others.
Technicians, service workers, machine operators and skilled craft workers	Lower writing index scores than clerical workers, managers, and professionals and higher scores than those in elementary occupations, but same scores as each other.
Elementary occupations	Lower writing intensity index values than all other occupations.

The skills of Canadian skilled craft workers were somewhat lower than those in similar occupations in Germany and the Netherlands, although they were somewhat higher than those in the United States (see Chapter 2). Table 3.5 compares the reading practices of workers in these occupations in Canada and other countries. Except for workers in Poland, Canadian skilled craft workers report doing less reading than their counterparts in the other IALS countries, including those in the United States. Whether employers organize work in Canada to meet the lower skill levels of their employees, or whether skilled craft workers in Canada have lower skills because the organization of their work provides them with little opportunity to practice their skill, or both, cannot be determined from the IALS data. This is, however, an important question that is raised by the IALS data, one with implications for the role of employers in maintaining Canada's skill base.

---

5.   It is important that these results be interpreted with caution. There may have been some type of text that workers in some occupations read with great frequency or some type of writing they do regularly, but which the IALS did not ask about. If this were the case, then the index would underestimate the relative standing of this occupation.

Reading the Future

The IALS data lead us to suggest that one of the characteristics of a "good job" ought to be the opportunities it provides to maintain and enhance skill. In this light, skilled craft jobs in Canada are not necessarily "good jobs," when compared with similar occupations in other countries.

In general, these observations suggest that one of the characteristics of a "good job" ought to be the opportunities it provides to maintain and enhance skill. In this light, jobs for skilled craft workers in Canada are not necessarily "good jobs" when compared with similar occupations in other countries. If highly skilled craft jobs are an important part of the high skill–high wages economy, then there is evidence from the comparatively low skills of those working in skilled craft jobs, and the low frequency of practices that characterizes their daily work, that Canada lags behind its major competitors. If Canada is to continue to attract a share of the world's high skill–high wage jobs, steps must be taken to improve both the skills of employees and the literacy opportunities afforded in the workplace.

Generally, Canadian workers reported less reading than their counterparts in other countries, with the general exception of Poland and with specific exceptions in comparison with the Netherlands. Skilled craft workers in Canada tend to have lower skill scores than those in other countries. Just what the relationship between low practice and low skill is cannot be fully investigated with the IALS data, but these results point to the merit of further research on this issue. The data do indicate that if good jobs are those that allow incumbents to enhance skills through practice, skilled craft jobs in Canada are not as "good" as skilled craft jobs in other countries.

Table 3.5

Comparison of skilled craft workers in Canada with those in other IALS countries using the proportion who engage in reading various tasks at least once a week, skilled craft workers aged 16 to 65

Skilled craft workers in	Do you read . . . at least once a week?				
	letters or memos	reports, articles, magazines or journals	manuals or reference books, including catalogues	diagrams or schematics	bills, invoices, spreadsheets or budget tables
			%		
Canada	43	30	37	48	33
Germany	69	43	59	73	54
Netherlands	38	37	51	40	23
Poland	17	11	13	29	8
Sweden	57	62	62	50	42
Switzerland (French)	54	62	55	56	57
Switzerland (German)	69	56	63	32	55
United States	53	39	53	58	35

The IALS data show that high skill is part of the change in the occupational mix in Canada. As Figure 3.1 shows, those occupations that have grown as part of the Canadian labour force since 1971 are those characterized by higher reading intensity scores. This parallels the finding that the occupational groups experiencing growth are those with relatively high literacy skills (see Chapter 2).

One of the high-growth occupational groups—service workers—does not have a high average reading intensity value, just as it has a relatively low average literacy ability score. This lends some support to claims that some areas of growth are not high skill and are, consequently, unlikely to be high wage. Indeed, the average annual salary was lowest for the service worker occupational group, though much of this is due to the high proportion of service workers who work part time.[6]

---

6.   Of the IALS respondents who were service workers, 46% reported working part time; the next highest part-time occupation was clerical workers, with 26% working part time.

A key finding of the IALS is the relatively large difference in the reading intensity indices between Level 1 and Level 2. This strongly suggests against grouping these levels in any analysis since what the people at these levels do, by way of literacy activities, and the literacy skills they possess, are quite distinct.

The scale used in this table is the scale most highly correlated with the task. For all tasks, those at higher literacy levels are more likely to report engaging in the task.

Figure 3.1

The relation between occupational change and reading intensity, Canadian adults aged 16 and over in the labour force

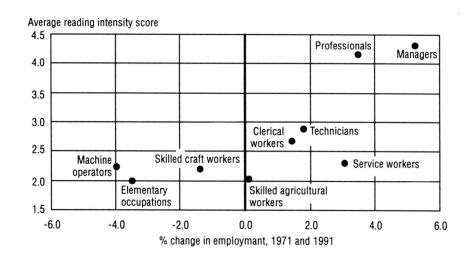

A key finding of the IALS, one which mirrors that found in LSUDA, is the relatively large difference in the reading intensity indices between Level 1 and Level 2, compared with the differences observed between the higher levels. Thus, Level 2 seems more like the level above it than the level below it and the difference between IALS Level 3 and IALS Level 4/5 is the smallest, except for bills and other monetary documents. This strongly suggests against grouping these levels in any analysis since what the people at these levels do, by way of literacy activities, and the literacy skills they possess, are quite distinct.

The sole exception to a relation between practice and skill is for measuring size and weight. Here the differences between levels are small. Of all the workplace literacy tasks covered in the IALS, measurement is the task with the highest proportion of Canadians at Level 1 reporting at least once a week frequency (40%). The occupational data on numeracy (Table 3.3), show that this task is more likely to be carried out by skilled craft workers and machine operators. As workers in these occupations tend to have lower literacy skills, it follows that this will lower the connection between skill and frequency for this task (Tables 3.6 through 3.8).[7]

Table 3.6

Proportion of respondents at each IALS literacy level who reported engaging in each of five workplace reading tasks at least once a week, Canadian adults aged 16 and over in the labour force

	Do you read . . . at least once a week?				
	letters or memos (Prose scale)	reports, articles, magazines or journals (Prose scale)	manuals or reference books, including catalogues (Document scale)	diagrams or schematics (Document scale)	bills, invoices, spreadsheets or budget tables (Document scale)
			%		
Level 1	35	25	22	14	25
Level 2	62	45	41	28	45
Level 3	76	60	51	34	50
Level 4/5	85	72	66	42	58

7. The test items that form the IALS quantitative scale include more items that reflect budget math than measurement math. This may also contribute to the low relationship between quantitative skill as measured in the IALS and reports of use of measurement on the job.

Table 3.7

Proportion of respondents at each IALS literacy level, document scale, who reported engaging in each of four workplace writing tasks at least once a week, Canadian adults aged 16 and over in the labour force

| | Do you write . . . at least once a week? | | | |
Document scale	letters or memos	forms or things such as bills, invoices or budgets	reports or articles	estimates or technical specifications
	%			
Level 1	28	24	18	18
Level 2	45	50	35	21
Level 3	55	48	43	27
Level 4/5	69	54	48	35

Table 3.8

Proportion of respondents by level, quantitative scale, who reported engaging in each of two workplace numeracy tasks at least once a week, Canadian adults aged 16 and over in the labour force

| | Do you use mathematics at least once a week to . . . | |
Quantitative scale	measure or estimate the size or weight of objects?	calculate prices, costs or budgets?
	%	
Level 1	40	23
Level 2	46	44
Level 3	49	52
Level 4/5	51	60

Table 3.9

Average scores and standard deviations by level, document scale level on a scale of reading and writing intensity (based on frequency and variety of tasks), Canadian adults aged 16 and over in the labour force

| | Reading and writing intensity scale | | | |
| | Reading intensity (maximum = 6) | | Writing intensity (maximum = 4) | |
Document scale	Mean	Standard deviation	Mean	Standard deviation
Level 1	1.4	1.8	0.9	1.3
Level 2	2.5	1.9	1.5	1.3
Level 3	2.9	1.8	1.7	1.5
Level 4/5	3.6	1.7	2.0	1.3

On the intensity indices, all four levels are distinct, indicating that higher skill is associated with both greater variety and greater frequency of reading and writing (Table 3.9). The data available in cross-sectional surveys such as the IALS do not allow investigation of causality, but it is likely that practice contributes to skill both through more frequent use of the skill and through greater variety by providing opportunities to use and expand the skill in new situations. Of course, skill contributes to practice by allowing individuals to enter and succeed in situations with opportunities for practice.

Self-perceptions of literacy skills

As well as the measured skill and the self-reported practices, the IALS collected data about respondents' perceptions of their own skills. Without a realistic sense of the adequacy of their own skills, Canadians may not make sound choices about participation in remedial education. The general pattern of responses differed little by scale; Table 3.10 contains the data for one scale for each of the three self-assessments.

Table 3.10

Percentage of respondents by level, prose, document and quantitative scales, who gave different ratings to their reading, writing and numeracy skills for work, Canadian adults aged 16 and over in the labour force

	How do you rate your . . . skills for your main job?				
			writing		
Prose scale	Excellent	Good	Moderate	Poor	No opinion
			%		
Level 1	17	27	17	24	15
Level 2	42	39	12	4	3
Level 3	52	35	9	...	4
Level 4/5	64	33	...	...	...
Overall	48	34	9	4	4

			reading		
Document scale	Excellent	Good	Moderate	Poor	No opinion
			%		
Level 1	22	27	15	16	20
Level 2	45	42	10	...	2
Level 3	65	26	6	...	...
Level 4/5	76	22	...	...	...
Overall	58	29	7	2	4

			mathematics		
Quantitative scale	Excellent	Good	Moderate	Poor	No opinion
			%		
Level 1	27	34	17	10	13
Level 2	32	47	12	...	7
Level 3	51	40	5	...	4
Level 4/5	60	31	...	...	...
Overall	46	38	9	2	5

... Sample size too small to produce reliable estimates.

Respondents at lower levels gave lower ratings, but a significant proportion of those at Level 1 nonetheless rated their skills as excellent. Overall only 2% of the respondents rated their skills as poor.

Most Canadian respondents felt their skills were at least good, though more at Level 1 rated them as moderate or poor or gave no opinion. At the same time, respondents at Level 4/5 were most likely to rate their skills as excellent and almost no one said their skills were poor. Overall, respondents were more likely to rate their reading skills as excellent than they were to give that rating to their writing or mathematical skills. While it may seem that individuals at Level 1 who say their skills are excellent are overrating their skills, this may not be the case; they were asked to relate their skills to their job demands. The IALS data on workplace literacy practices in Canada demonstrate that the demands for some individuals are low; in these situations even low skills would be satisfactory. Of those at Level 1 who work, 44% reported that there was no reading task they did at least once a week; only 4% at this level said they did all the reading tasks at least once a week.[8] In contrast, only 15% of Level 2 workers, 11% of Level 3 workers, but 4% of Level 4 workers said they did none of the tasks.[9]

---

8. It must also be remembered that Level 1 includes a range of ability and it should be expected that those who rate their skills as excellent are those at the upper end of this range; in fact, that is the case. Though the number of respondents is too small for a complete analysis by level, the average document scores of the Level 1 respondents with self-ratings of excellent are significantly higher than the document scores of the Level 1 respondents who gave lower self-ratings ($df = 374$, $t = 373$, $p < .001$).

9. This is yet another illustration of how Level 1 is different from Level 2, in a way that Level 2 is not different from Level 3.

Table 3.11 has a comparison of the reading and writing intensity scores for each of the self-rating categories. Individuals who gave themselves higher ratings also did more reading and writing. This may be because people who have greater confidence in their skills, such as those who rated their skills as excellent, expect to be able to access print for information and do so, while those with less confidence, such as those who rated their skills as poor, do not use texts because they do not expect to be successful. Individuals who rated their skills as excellent but were at Level 1 did less reading than those at higher levels who rated their skills the same (Table 3.12), an additional indication that the self-ratings of skills for work, even when Level 1 respondents rate their skills as excellent, may reflect the relative match between skills and demand more than some absolute rating of skills. However, as Table 3.12 also shows, there is little difference in writing intensity by level for those who said their reading skills were excellent. This may be because the IALS skill measures are measures of reading and not writing and, thus, do not capture differences in the latter skill, though it is unlikely that there are many adults whose writing skills are superior to their reading skills.[10]

Individuals who rated their skills higher are more likely to engage in a wider variety of reading or writing tasks frequently.

Table 3.11

Relation between self-perception and intensity of reading and writing at work, Canadian adults aged 16 and over in the labour force

| | Reading and writing intensity scale | | | |
| | Reading intensity (maximum = 6) | | Writing intensity (maximum = 4) | |
Self-rating of skill	Mean	Standard deviation	Mean	Standard deviation
Excellent	3.2	1.8	2.0	1.4
Good	2.8	1.9	1.6	1.3
Moderate	2.0	1.7	1.2	1.3
Poor	0.9	1.2	0.5	0.8
No opinion	0.2	0.7	0.2	0.5

Individuals at higher skill levels have higher reading intensity scores, suggesting that respondents are making a relative judgment ("How well do my skills fit the demands I face?") rather than an absolute one ("How good are my skills?"). The writing intensity scores do not differ by level, but that may be because document scale levels are a poor proxy for writing skills (prose and quantitative scale levels provide an even poorer fit between the intensity scale and the estimate of ability).

Table 3.12

Relation between self-perception and intensity of reading and writing at work for those who rated their skill for their main job as excellent, Canadian adults aged 16 and over in the labour force

| | Reading and writing intensity scale | | | |
| | Reading intensity (maximum = 6) | | Writing intensity (maximum = 4) | |
Document scale (Self-rating of skills for work is excellent)	Mean	Standard deviation	Mean	Standard deviation
Level 1	2.5	2.0	1.9	1.6
Level 2	2.8	1.9	1.8	1.5
Level 3	3.1	1.8	1.9	1.5
Level 4/5	3.6	1.6	2.2	1.3

10. The lack of differentiation by level in Table 3.12 may not come from the IALS scale scores underestimating the writing skills of those at Level 1 on the document scale, but from overestimating the writing skills of those at the higher levels.

Skills as a barrier to job change

Respondents who were in the labour force were also asked whether their literacy skills were a barrier to finding a job or moving to a better job. The overall results by literacy scale levels are in Table 3.13. The number who said their skills are limiting represent about the same proportion of the population as those who said their skills for their main job were poor or moderate. That is because they are often the same people. As Table 3.14 shows, those who rate their skills as poor or moderate were considerably more likely to say this limits their job opportunities. Typically, those who evaluated their skills as poor were more likely to say they were greatly limiting, while those who evaluated their skills as moderate were more likely to say this was only somewhat limiting. These results suggest that only a minority of those with low skills, whether self-identified or measured by the IALS test, see any need to improve their skills. This fact is of great concern for public policy, since without awareness of the need to improve, few Canadians will seek opportunities to enhance their skills.

Table 3.13

Proportion of respondents by level, prose, document and quantitative scales, who reported how limiting they found their reading, writing and numeracy skills for work, Canadian adults aged 16 and over in the labour force

	To what extent are your . . . skills limiting your job opportunity?		
		writing	
Prose scale	Greatly limiting	Somewhat limiting	Not imiting
		%	
Level 1	16	19	64
Level 2	...	13	82
Level 3	...	8	91
Level 4/5	...	3	98
Overall	4	9	87
		reading	
Document scale	Greatly limiting	Somewhat limiting	Not limiting
		%	
Level 1	13	27	60
Level 2	...	12	84
Level 3	...	6	92
Level 4/5	...	...	99
Overall	3	9	88
		mathematics	
Quantitative scale	Greatly limiting	Somewhat limiting	Not limiting
		%	
Level 1	12	22	66
Level 2	...	17	81
Level 3	...	8	91
Level 4/5	...	...	97
Overall	2	11	87

...   Sample size too small to produce reliable estimates.

Table 3.14

Proportion of each self-rating group who reported how limiting they found their reading, writing and numeracy skills for work, Canadian adults aged 16 and over in the labour force

	To what extent are your . . . skills limiting your job opportunities?		
	reading		
Self-assessment	Greatly limiting	Somewhat limiting	Not limiting
	%		
Excellent	...	1	97
Good	...	12	86
Moderate	...	47	50
Poor	38	...	...
	writing		
Self-assessment	Greatly limiting	Somewhat limiting	Not limiting
	%		
Excellent	...	2	98
Good	...	9	89
Moderate	...	48	49
Poor	43	16	41
	mathematics		
Self-assessment	Greatly limiting	Somewhat limiting	Not limiting
	%		
Excellent	...	2	98
Good	...	17	82
Moderate	...	29	70
Poor	48	...	...

...   Sample size too small to produce reliable estimates.

Those who rated their skills as poor are more likely than others to see them as greatly limiting, while those who rated their skills as moderate are more likely to see them as only somewhat limiting.

Reading outside the workplace

Literacy does not occur exclusively in work settings, of course; some of the most important uses of literacy are part of everyday life. The IALS also asked respondents about their use of literacy skill in everyday activities outside the workplace.[11] One set of questions paralleled the workplace reading tasks questions (Table 3.15). The relationship between skill and practice here is slightly different than in the workplace questions. While a smaller proportion of those at Level 1 reported engaging in every task at least once a week, the differences among Levels 2, 3 and 4/5 are notably smaller for the daily tasks than for the workplace ones. This may be because the ordinary demands of daily literacy are less than those at work, so that Level 2 is adequate for most circumstances. The reading intensity scale for daily reading (constructed from the daily reading task questions in the same fashion as the workplace intensity scale is constructed from the workplace tasks) shows how similar Levels 2, 3 and 4/5 are and how different they are from Level 1 (Table 3.16).[12]

11.   In order to contain response burden, most of the IALS countries chose not to ask questions about daily reading outside the workplace. Consequently, little comparative data are available.

12.   The intensity differences are statistically significant ($df = 3, 5558, F = 225.7, p < .001$). Because of the large sample size, even small differences are statistically significant and the post hoc analysis, using the Newman–Keuls procedure, shows that each level is distinct from the others on the reading intensity index.

Table 3.15

Proportion of respondents by level who reported engaging in each of six daily reading tasks at least once a week, Canadian adults aged 16 and over

	Do you read . . . at least once a week?					
	letters or memos (Prose scale)	reports, articles, magazines or journals (Document scale)	manuals or reference books, including catalogues (Document) scale)	diagrams or schematics (Document scale)	bills, invoices, spreadsheets or budget tables (Document scale)	directions or instructions for medicines, recipes or other products (Prose scale)
				%		
Level 1	32	41	24	5	34	37
Level 2	51	67	49	15	52	53
Level 3	55	69	53	21	60	54
Level 4/5	59	78	55	23	69	62

Table 3.16

Average scores and standard deviations by level, document scale level on a scale of reading intensity (based on frequency and variety of everyday tasks), Canadian adults aged 16 and over

	Reading intensity scale	
	Reading intensity (maximum = 6)	
Document scale	Mean	Standard deviation
Level 1	1.8	1.6
Level 2	2.9	1.7
Level 3	3.1	1.8
Level 4/5	3.4	1.6

Fewer individuals at Level 1 reported engaging in these tasks, but the differences between Levels 2, 3 and 4/5 are quite small, especially when compared with similar tasks in the workplace (Table 3.6).

Each higher level has a significantly higher score on the intensity scale (df = 3, 5558, F = 225.7, p < .001).

Reading the newspaper is one of the most common events in everyday life. Most Canadians, as do most of their counterparts in the other countries, said they read a newspaper, if not every day, at least once a week (Table 3.17). But not all read the paper the same way. Individuals at different prose levels report quite different patterns when asked about specific sections of the newspaper (Table 3.18).[13] With a few exceptions (television listings being the most notable one), individuals at higher literacy levels were more likely to report reading a section of the newspaper than those at a lower level. There are a small group of sections (advertisements, local news, sports, horoscopes and advice columns) where there is little difference between Levels 2, 3 and 4/5, though all three have a higher frequency than Level 1. It is not useful to speculate why certain newspaper sections show a greater differentiation by level than others, though the differences in education among the levels may play a role.

13. The prose scale levels are used to avoid a complex table. The results using the document and quantitative scales yield virtually identical patterns.

Table 3.17

Comparisons of newspaper reading frequency in the IALS countries, adults aged 16 to 65

	How often do you read a newspaper?	
	Every day	At least once a week
	%	
Canada	59	87
Germany	83	97
Netherlands	79	95
Poland	60	89
Sweden	90	99
Switzerland (French)	77	94
Switzerland (German)	78	99
United States	62	85

Fewer Canadians reported reading a newspaper every day, but the number reading a paper at least once a week (which includes those who read daily) is more like the pattern in the other countries. Patterns in the United States and Canada are very similar.

Table 3.18

Proportions of respondents by level, prose scale, who reported reading each of 15 sections of a newspaper, Canadian adults aged 16 and over who reported reading a newspaper regularly

	Which parts of the newspaper do you generally read?				
Prose scale	Classified ads	Other ads	National or international news	Regional or local news	Sports
	%				
Level 1	48	49	62	74	33
Level 2	65	67	76	92	49
Level 3	58	65	82	94	49
Level 4/5	55	66	88	95	47

Prose scale	Home, fashion, health	Editorials	Financial news	Comics	Television listings
	%				
Level 1	42	39	16	31	49
Level 2	60	54	29	47	51
Level 3	64	65	40	50	50
Level 4/5	72	73	46	57	39

Prose scale	Movie or concert listings	Book or movie reviews	Horoscope	Advice columns	Other
	%				
Level 1	34	16	39	30	9
Level 2	50	38	56	49	13
Level 3	59	54	50	41	14
Level 4/5	69	69	45	46	16

Some sections, such as national or international news and editorials, show a marked effect by level; others (television listings, for example) show no effect by level. In other cases, a smaller proportion of readers fall into Level 1, but the other levels do not differ (regional and local news).

The IALS evidence concerning the use of literacy materials in the home, as from the other questions about daily activities, is that Level 1 does not reflect an absence of literacy activities, but a lower level of them. In fundamental literacy matters—reading newspapers, consulting dictionaries—individuals at Level 1 have a high participation rate.

Other questions asked about other kinds of literacy activities in the home: those more concerned with reading books. One group (Table 3.19) inquired about literacy materials in the home. As in all the other indicators of literacy activities, those at higher levels were more likely to report having the reading materials than those at lower levels. However, the reading materials are not completely absent in the homes of those in Level 1. Many have a weekly source of news (a magazine or a newspaper); almost 50% report owning 25 or more books, and almost all have a dictionary. The IALS evidence concerning the use of literacy materials in the home, as from the other questions about daily activities, is that Level 1 does not reflect an absence of literacy activities, but a lower level of them. In fundamental literacy matters—reading newspapers, consulting dictionaries—individuals at Level 1 have a high participation rate; it is in the use of more complex resources such as encyclopedias that differences by level are accentuated.

Levels 2, 3 and 4/5 are similar, but the homes of those at Level 1 are less likely to contain these materials.

Canadians do not appear less "literate" than others in comparisons of daily literacy practice outside of the workplace. Neither do young adults appear to engage in daily literacy tasks any less frequently than older adults.

Table 3.19

Proportion of respondents by level, prose scale, who reported having each of five types of literacy materials in their home, Canadian adults aged 16 and over

Prose scale	Do you currently have . . . in your home?				
	a daily newspaper	a weekly news-paper/magazine	more than 25 books	an encyclopedia	a dictionary
			%		
Level 1	50	68	50	35	80
Level 2	66	78	80	51	89
Level 3	69	81	91	58	97
Level 4/5	63	79	97	56	96

A small group of questions about literacy activities outside work were included in the IALS (Table 3.20). These practices overlap with those discussed above, but they provide the only comparative picture on daily literacy. Across all countries, the same pattern that is found in all the Canadian data appears: a larger proportion of those at Level 4/5 report engaging in literacy activities outside work than do those at each lower level.

Canadians do not appear less "literate" than others in these comparisons. There is no clear pattern in which Canadian adults consistently did less reading or writing than adults in some other countries. Level 1 Canadians were less likely to read a newspaper than Level 1 adults elsewhere, except those in the United States, but they wrote letters about as often as Level 1 adults in the Netherlands and Sweden. Adults in Canada at Level 4/5 read books somewhat more frequently than those in most countries, but they typically wrote letters less often. In general, these data suggest that adults in Canada practice daily literacy much as adults in the United States do. The patterns of the two countries are quite similar.

Table 3.20

Proportion of respondents by level, prose scale, who reported engaging in each of four literacy tasks in each IALS country, adults aged 16 to 65

		Do you . . .			
		read newspapers at least once a week?	read books at least once a week?	write letters at least once a week?	visit a library at least once a month?
			%		
Canada	Level 1	69	29	11	13
	Level 2	92	41	16	17
	Level 3	91	54	18	27
	Level 4/5	92	75	25	40
Germany	Level 1	91	35	13	13
	Level 2	97	42	17	15
	Level 3	98	50	26	23
	Level 4/5	97	64	27	36
Netherlands	Level 1	88	25	9	15
	Level 2	94	37	14	27
	Level 3	97	49	21	42
	Level 4/5	96	60	26	46
Poland	Level 1	83	25	6	11
	Level 2	94	41	15	22
	Level 3	97	56	23	32
	Level 4/5	98	79	40	46
Sweden	Level 1	95	35	10	20
	Level 2	98	42	10	23
	Level 3	99	51	12	32
	Level 4/5	99	64	19	44
Switzerland (French)	Level 1	95	40	14	13
	Level 2	94	49	20	14
	Level 3	98	62	33	20
	Level 4/5	100	66	40	32
Switzerland (German)	Level 1	92	37	16	5
	Level 2	97	46	21	11
	Level 3	97	62	28	20
	Level 4/5	97	83	37	32
United States	Level 1	67	34	15	13
	Level 2	89	46	17	18
	Level 3	92	57	22	29
	Level 4/5	97	60	24	35

The pattern in Canada is similar to that in other countries.

Because the international comparisons in Table 3.20 include only those aged 16 to 65, Table 3.21 includes the same questions for the full adult population 16 and over surveyed in Canada. The only task in which there is any significant difference between the 16-to-65 age group and the total adult population is for writing letters. This suggests that for this task at least there may be an age effect.

Table 3.21

Proportion of each prose level who reported regular participation in various literacy and literacy-related activities, Canadian adults aged 16 and over

	Do you . . .				
Prose scale	read news-papers at least once a week?	read books at least once a week?	write letters at least once a month?	visit a library at least once a month?	participate in volunteer activi-ties at least once a month?
	%				
Level 1	70	30	19	10	12
Level 2	92	43	36	17	19
Level 3	92	56	42	29	25
Level 4/5	92	75	48	40	40

Table 3.22 presents the results for these questions by age group. Young adults did not appear to engage in literacy tasks any less frequently than older adults. They visited libraries more often, but that is likely because many are still in school, and they were more frequent letter writers. The differences are not large, except that those over 65 have significantly the lowest use.[14] Smith (1996) found a similar lack of an age effect in the United States in his analysis of similar data from the National Adult Literacy Survey. A widespread assumption that young adults are less involved with literacy is not generally supported by the data from these national surveys.

Table 3.22

Proportion of respondents in different age groups who reported engaging in each of six daily reading tasks at least once a week, Canadian adults aged 16 and over

	Do you read . . . at least once a week?					
Age group	letters or memos	reports, articles, magazines or journals	manuals or reference books, including catalogues	diagrams or schematics	bills, invoices, spreadsheets or budget tables	directions or instructions for medicines, recipes or other products
	%					
16 to 25	49	67	53	21	38	43
26 to 35	51	62	44	14	62	53
36 to 45	55	65	52	20	64	58
46 to 55	57	73	50	20	68	52
56 to 65	45	65	46	14	48	51
Over 65	37	51	28	9	35	51

---

14. $df = 5, 5556, F = 41.8, p < .001$.

Statistics Canada – Catalogue no. 89-551-XPE

Literacy and television

Another widely held belief is that the growth in time spent watching television has led to a decline in literacy skills. Certainly the IALS data support the view that there is a strong association between literacy skill and the amount of time spent watching television (Table 3.23). Canadian adults with lower skills are more likely to spend two or more hours per day watching television. Some may be tempted to see the time spent with television as a cause of lower skills, but it is just as plausible to see the lower skills leading to more viewing time. Those with low skills may not be able to get the information they need from print, simply because of their low skills, and may turn to television instead. Table 3.24 compares the proportion of adults at each level who said they get a lot of information from television with the proportion who said they get a lot from newspapers. Fewer Level 1 adults said that newspapers were the source for a lot of their information and fewer Level 4/ 5 adults said that television was such a source. Table 3.23 also shows that while slightly more young adults watched television extensively (more than two hours a day) than those in the middle adult age group (from 26 to 55), this is markedly smaller than the proportion of those 55 and over who watched this frequently.

This is consistent with the results from Statistics Canada's 1986 National Survey of Time Use.[15] That survey found that the average number of hours spent watching television for those 65 and over was 3.3, while for those under 25 it was 2.0. The difference is due in large part to the greater number of hours of free time those 65 and over have (7.7 hours a day) compared with those under 25 (5.4). Another reason individuals with low literacy skills may watch more television is simply that they have more time to do so. Because those with low skills are less likely to be employed, they are likely to have more free time. The time use survey also estimated that individuals looking for work had more than three hours more free time each day than those who were employed (7.7 hours versus 4.5, respectively) and that they watched just over 1.5 more hours of television (3.5 versus 1.9). Interestingly though, the extra free time did not result in more reading by those looking for work. There was little difference in the time spent reading between the two groups (0.3 hours each day for those looking for work versus 0.4 hours for employed), and that difference was due to different proportions of each gender in the two groups, as men who were employed or looking for work read the same (0.4 hours) as did employed and looking-for-work women (0.3 hours each day).

Table 3.23

Proportion of respondents by level, document scale, and each age group who reported watching television at least five hours or more and two hours or more (including those watching five or more), Canadian adults aged 16 and over

	Television watching Hours per day	
	Two or more	Five or more
	%	
Document scale		
Level 1	58	18
Level 2	45	8
Level 3	39	4
Level 4/5	26	2
Age group		
16 to 25	44	6
26 to 35	38	5
36 to 45	34	4
46 to 55	34	6
56 to 65	55	17
Over 65	62	16

15. *Where does time go?* General Social Survey Analysis Series, No. 4, Harvey et al. 1991.

Table 3.24

Proportion of respondents by level, prose scale, who identified television and newspapers as major sources of information, Canadian adults aged 16 and over

Prose scale	Do you get a lot of information from . . .	
	newspapers?	television?
	%	
Level 1	26	71
Level 2	42	69
Level 3	52	70
Level 4/5	49	48

A smaller proportion of respondents at Level 1 said they get a lot of information from newspapers and a smaller proportion of respondents at Level 4/5 said they get a lot from television.

Self-perceptions of literacy skills outside of work

The IALS also asked adults about their perceptions of their own literacy skills for everyday reading outside of work. As Table 3.25 shows, here too adults at lower levels were more likely to think that their skills are poor, with 20% of those at Level 1 saying their reading skills were poor. And here too, respondents were more likely to give their writing and mathematics skills lower scores. Those who gave themselves higher ratings were those who did more reading (Table 3.26).

Table 3.25

Proportion of respondents by level, prose, document and quantitative scales, who gave different evaluations to their literacy skills for everyday activities

	How do you rate your . . . skills for daily life?			
	writing			
Prose scale	Excellent	Good	Moderate	Poor
	%			
Level 1	10	32	27	30
Level 2	36	45	13	7
Level 3	53	38	8	...
Level 4/5	72	26	...	...
Overall	**44**	**36**	**12**	**8**

	reading			
Document scale	Excellent	Good	Moderate	Poor
	%			
Level 1	25	32	24	20
Level 2	44	46	8	...
Level 3	69	28	3	...
Level 4/5	81	18	...	...
Overall	**56**	**31**	**8**	**5**

	mathematics			
Quantitative scale	Excellent	Good	Moderate	Poor
	%			
Level 1	16	42	26	16
Level 2	32	47	17	4
Level 3	53	39	7	...
Level 4/5	67	26	...	...
Overall	**43**	**39**	**14**	**5**

... Sample size too small to produce reliable estimates.

Individuals with lower skills are more likely to assess their skills as poor, but some at this level rated their skills as excellent.

Table 3.26

Average scores and standard deviations for self-assessment category on a scale of reading intensity (based on frequency and variety of everyday tasks), Canadian adults aged 16 and over

	Reading intensity scale Reading intensity (maximum = 6)	
Self-rating of skill	Mean	Standard deviation
Excellent	3.3	1.7
Good	2.6	1.7
Moderate	1.9	1.5
Poor	1.2	1.4

People who rated their skills higher have corresponding higher reading intensity scores (df = 3, 5472, F = 200.0, p < .001).

In general, the picture of adult daily reading outside work is much the same as that for the workplace. Whether it be at work or in daily life outside work, highly skilled individuals read, write and calculate more or, to suggest a different causal relationship, those who read, write and calculate more have higher literacy skills. The workplace may be important to literacy because it is a site where it may be more difficult to avoid literacy tasks. Only 38% of the adults for whom both workplace and home reading intensity scores are available had higher home intensity scores, suggesting that for a substantial majority the workplace provided as many (26%) or more (37%) reading opportunities than home.

Chapter 4

Measuring the success of the IALS

Jean Pignal
National Study Manager, Statistics Canada

R eaders should be left with little doubt that literacy is central to the well-being of both individuals and nations. The evidence presented in this report provides a portrait of Canadian literacy that adds much to our understanding of the impact and benefits of literacy in modern economies and societies. Little would be gained by repeating the many and varied findings presented in the preceding substantive chapters. In concluding, it is more useful to return to the objectives of the IALS, to illustrate how they have been met.

First, the IALS study[1] provides unique comparative data for an interesting cross-section of Canada's competitors. The IALS dataset currently represents more than 277 million people from six of our key trading partners: the United States, Germany, the Netherlands, Sweden, Switzerland and Poland. Together, these countries account for more than 70% of our import trade and 82% of our exports.[2] Moreover, the IALS has attracted interest and support from organizations such as the Organisation for Economic Co-operation and Development and the European Union—interest that has encouraged more countries to field this study. If we accept that literacy is important, then our position relative to these countries is crucial to Canada's economic success. The findings presented in Chapters 1, 2 and 3 clearly demonstrate both comparative strengths and weaknesses. These data will permit policy makers to continue building on our strengths and, more importantly, will allow them to concentrate scarce resources in areas that may be amenable to intervention by individuals, employers and governments.

Second, the IALS study also provides an updated profile of Canadian adult literacy skills that enable comparison to those of the LSUDA survey. While the levels are not directly comparable on a one-to-one basis, this is a minor inconvenience compared with the benefits of the improved testing technology adopted in the IALS design. The linkage to the LSUDA levels presented in Chapter 1 shows little change in the literacy profiles in Canada in the past five years. This comparison belies predictions of the failure of the school system and a continuing erosion of literacy skills in Canada. At the same time, given that a new cohort graduated from secondary school in the intervening period, one might have expected some improvement. In fact, these latest graduates **are** generally more literate than the older cohorts ahead of them. Evidently, other factors must be working to alter the literacy skill profile of the labour force. The findings of this Canadian report indicate that changes in Canada's stock of literacy skills are the product of complex social and economic forces. These forces mediate the supply

---

1. *Literacy, Economy and Society: Results of the first International Adult Literacy Survey*, Organisation for Economic Co-operation and Development and Statistics Canada 1995.

2. *Exports, merchandise trade*, Statistics Canada 1996 and *Imports, merchandise trade*, Statistics Canada 1996.

of, and the demand for, skills in general and literacy in particular. The increasing demand for more highly skilled workers assumes an adequate matching supply. Such supply cannot be taken for granted.

Third, the study provides data for special subpopulations that the LSUDA identified as being of particular interest to policy makers, including Unemployment Insurance beneficiaries, social assistance recipients, youth in and out of school, seniors, and specific linguistic minorities in Ontario and New Brunswick. Human Resources Development Canada and others have commissioned a series of studies that will advance our understanding of these special subpopulations—all of which deserve individual attention. Furthermore, the richness of the dataset will undoubtedly generate much research, providing further insights into the determinants and consequences of literacy in Canada.

Fourth, the study sheds light on the relationship between performance, educational attainment, labour market participation and employment of those individuals found to be at IALS Level 2. Analysis of the 1989 LSUDA results found this level, more or less equivalent to the LSUDA's Level 3, to be of particular interest. The IALS confirms that this level is distinct. The data show that, while not highly literate, members of this group generally feel comfortable, both at work and at home, with their skills. They do not feel hindered by their skills nor do they see the need for remedial assistance to better them. Such results would not be remarkable if it were not for the changing demands of occupations. Workers are increasingly being asked to complete tasks previously mastered by others who may have possessed higher literacy skills. Restructuring has transformed work organizations so that they now require complex decisions at all levels—decisions that require all workers to have greater access to information. While skills at Level 2 may be adequate for present demands in their workplace, the future demands of that same workplace may be more rigorous.

Fifth, the IALS study was also designed to test the notion that decoding and decision-making skills embodied in the Canadian and American assessments, such as the Young Adult Literacy Survey, the Survey of Literacy Skills Used in Daily Activities, the Department of Labor Literacy Survey and the National Adult Literacy Survey, are stable across language groups and cultures. The IALS broke new ground in understanding literacy and its distribution, and has dispelled most reservations about the potential for comparing literacy proficiency across languages and cultures. The richness and validity of the data obtained exceeded even the expectations of the project's most enthusiastic supporters. In short, the study proves to be a remarkable scientific advance.

The IALS demonstrates that modern measurement technology is capable of making valid estimates of adults' abilities across countries. Both the theories of literacy and the measurement scales devised in national contexts have proved robust when adapted to multiple languages and cultures. For the first time, the competencies of different countries' adult populations could be reliably compared. Such a breakthrough will have implications beyond the measurement of literacy. In a world in which the work force's abilities are thought to be crucial in determining well-being and economic performance, the demand for such knowledge is immense.

Sixth, the study attempts to promote the concept of literacy underlying the direct assessments conducted in Canada and the United States. This, and the previous international report based on the IALS, contains information on seven countries including Canada. In addition, data has also been collected in Ireland,[3] the United Kingdom, New Zealand, Australia and the Flemish community in Belgium. Moreover, 15 additional countries plan to field the survey in the fall of

---

3. Data for Ireland were collected along with the original seven IALS countries, but were not ready for inclusion in the IALS report.

1997. Once complete, IALS data will be available for virtually every OECD country, and will represent a large percentage of the world's economy. If volume means anything, it would appear that the IALS has more than met this objective, and its success lies in being able to predict both the ability of a population and the difficulty of a cognitive task. With this information, nations can develop thoughtful policies based on observable and verifiable findings. The IALS model provides a liberating framework that has helped to shape the public discourse about literacy. No longer do we speak of literates versus illiterates—or haves and have nots. We can now speak about levels of literacy with each level capable of supporting a broad spectrum of analysis. It is unfortunate that seven years after LSUDA first operationalized these concepts in Canada, some cognitive dissonance continues to manifest itself with the old concepts of literacy being mixed in with the new. In answer to this, if the IALS were to adopt a mantra, it might be "Level 1 [is not] an absence of literacy activities, but a lower level of them."

The final goal of the IALS study was to compare and contrast the literacy skill profiles for economically important subpopulations among countries and language groups. Again the IALS data have exceeded all expectations. The economic structure and organization of all seven participating countries varied considerably. They have different industrial and occupational structures, varying degrees of rigidity or flexibility in their labor markets, and different labour market policies, industrial strategies, education systems and demographic structures. These variations have allowed an exploration of the factors that are amenable to policy intervention in a manner previously impossible. In short, the IALS has allowed us to see the footprints of policy in the distribution of literacy found in other countries.

This report is not the final word on the IALS data. Like any good study, it raises as many interesting questions as it answers. Some of these questions should be addressed in thematic reports now in preparation. In addition, data from several other countries will soon enrich the IALS dataset, and further data collection initiatives for specific Canadian subpopulations are also being planned. The development of similar technology to measure a broader range of skills, such as problem-solving, writing skills and oral communication, is a current priority if we are to understand the relationship of literacy to other skills and to the productivity of firms and national economies.

Literacy is important: it rewards those who are proficient and penalizes those who are not. For the individual, literacy affects employment success, income and life chances: literacy is both enriching and empowering. For countries, it does this by providing the labour force needed to maintain the competitive advantages required by this, increasingly global, village.

References

Barnow, B. "The impact of CETA programmes on earnings: A review of the literature." *Journal of Human Resources,* (22, 1987): 157–193.

Björklund, A. "Evaluation of labour market policy in Sweden." In *Evaluating Labour Market and Social Programmes: The State of a Complex Art,* pp. 73–88. Paris: OECD, 1991.

Björklund, A. and R. Moffitt. "The estimation of wage gains and welfare gains in self-selection models." *The Review of Economics and Statistics,* (64, 1987): 42–49.

Council of Ministers of Education Canada. *Technical report: Mathematics assessment 1993,* School Achievement Indicators Program. Toronto: Council of Ministers of Education Canada, 1994.

Council of Ministers of Education Canada. *Technical report: Reading and writing assessment,* School Achievement Indicators Program. Toronto: Council of Ministers of Education Canada, 1995.

The Creative Research Group. *Literacy in Canada: a research report* (Prepared for Southam News, Ottawa). Toronto, 1987.

Elley, Warwick B., ed. *The International Association for the Evaluation of Educational Achievement (IEA) Study of Reading Literacy: Achievement and Instruction in Thirty-two School Systems.* Oxford: Pergamon Press, 1994.

Freeman, Richard B., ed. *Working under different rules,* NBER Project Report. New York: Russell Sage Foundation, 1994.

Harvey, Andrew S., Katherine Marshall and Judith A. Frederick. *Where does time go?* General Social Survey Analysis Series, No. 4. (Statistics Canada Catalogue no. 11-612-MPE.) Ottawa: Minister of Industry, Science and Technology, 1991.

Jones, Stan. *Reading, but not reading well: Reading skills at Level 3.* Ottawa: National Literacy Secretariat, 1993.

Kirsch, Irwin S. and Ann Jungeblut. *Literacy: Profiles of America's Young Adults.* Princeton, N.J.: Educational Testing Service, 1986.

Kirsch, Irwin S., Ann Jungeblut and Anne Campbell. *Beyond the School Doors: The Literacy Needs of Job Seekers Served by the U.S. Department of Labor.* Washington, D.C.: U.S. Department of Labor, 1992.

Kirsch, Irwin S., Ann Jungeblut, Lynn Jenkins and Andrew Kolstad. *Adult Literacy in America: A First Look at the Results of the National Adult Literacy Survey.* Washington, D.C.: National Center for Education Statistics, U.S. Department of Education, 1993.

Lothian, Trudy. *Something for Seniors: Evaluation report 3 on an adult literacy program for seniors.* Ottawa: Carleton University, 1992.

Lothian, Trudy and Stan Jones. *Something Special for Seniors: Evaluation report 1 on an adult literacy program for seniors.* Ottawa: Carleton University, 1991.

Moffitt, R. "Incentive effects of the US welfare system: A review." *Journal of Economic Literature,* (30, 1992): 1–61.

Mosenthal, Peter B. and Irwin S. Kirsch. "Toward an explanatory model of document literacy." *Discourse Processes* (14, 1991): 147–180.

National Anti-Poverty Organization. *Literacy and Poverty—A View from the Inside.* Ottawa: February 1993.

Ontario Ministry of Education and Training. *Enquête internationale sur l'alphabétisation des adultes, rapport sur la composante francophone de l'Ontario.* Toronto: Ontario Ministry of Education and Training (in press).

Organisation for Economic Co-operation and Development. *The OECD Jobs Study: Evidence and Explanations, Parts I and II.* Paris: OECD, 1994.

Organisation for Economic Co-operation and Development and Statistics Canada. *Literacy, Economy and Society: Results of the first International Adult Literacy Survey.* Ottawa: OECD and Minister of Industry, 1995.

Organisation for Economic Co-operation and Development. "Transitions to learning economies and societies." In *Lifelong Learning for All*, pp. 29–70. Paris: OECD, 1996.

Riddell, C. "Evaluation of manpower and training programmes: The North American experience." In *Evaluating Labour Market and Social Programmes: The State of a Complex Art*, pp. 43–73. Paris: OECD, 1991.

Riddell, W. Craig. *Evidence on the Effectiveness of Youth Labour Market Programs in Canada: An Assessment.* Ottawa: Social Research and Demonstration Program, 1996.

Ridder, G. "An event history approach to the evaluation of training, recruitment and employment programmes." *Journal of Applied Econometrics,* (1, 1986): 109–126.

Smith, Jacquie and Michael Marsiske. "Definitions and Taxonomy of Foundation Skills and Adult Competences: Life Span Perspectives." In A. Tuijnman, I. Kirsch and D. Wagner, eds. *Adult Basic Skills: Innovations in Measurement and Policy Analysis.* Cresskill, N.J.: Hampton Press, 1996.

Smith, M. Cecil. "Differences in adults' reading practices and literacy proficiencies." *Reading Research Quarterly*, (31, 1996): 196–219.

Stanovich, K.E. "Matthew effects in reading: Some consequences of individual differences in the acquisition of literacy." *Reading Research Quarterly,* (21, 1986): 360–407.

Statistics Canada. *Adult Literacy in Canada: Results of a National Study.* (Statistics Canada Catalogue no. 89-525-XPE.) Ottawa: Minister of Industry, Science and Technology, 1991.

Statistics Canada. *An International Assessment of Adult Literacy: A Proposal.* Ottawa: Minister of Industry, Science and Technology, 1992.

Statistics Canada. *Leaving school: results from a national survey comparing school leavers and high school graduates 18 to 20 years of age.* (Statistics Canada Catalogue no. 81-575-XPE.) Ottawa: Minister of Supply and Services Canada, 1993.

Statistics Canada. *Educational attainment and school attendance: The nation (1991 Census).* (Statistics Canada Catalogue no. 93-328-XPB.) Ottawa: Minister of Industry, Science and Technology, 1993.

Statistics Canada. *The 1992 Adult Education and Training Survey.* Ottawa: Human Resources Development Canada and Statistics Canada, 1995.

Statistics Canada. *Exports, merchandise trade.* (Statistics Canada Catalogue no. 65-202-XPB.) Ottawa: Minister of Industry, 1996.

Statistics Canada. *Imports, merchandise trade.* (Statistics Canada Catalogue no. 65-203-XPB.) Ottawa: Minister of Industry, 1996.

U.S. Department of Education. *Adult Literacy: An International Perspective.* Washington: 1996.

UNESCO. *The Emergence of Learning Societies: Who Participates in Adult Learning* (in press).

Yamamoto, Kentaro and Irwin S. Kirsch. *Estimating Literacy Proficiencies With and Without Cognitive Data.* Princeton, N.J.: Educational Testing Service, 1993.

Appendix A

Participants

Statistics Canada IALS Team

Danielle Baum
Linda Bélanger
Yves Bélanger
Sylvie Blais
Colleen Bolger
Claire Bradshaw
Debbie Calcutt
Adriana Cargnello
Nancy Darcovich
Huguette Demers
Ron Dubeau
John Flanders
Lia Gendron
Stan Jones, Consultant
Sylvain Juneau
Paul Labelle
Claude Lafleur
Anna Maneiro
Scott Murray
David Neice, Consultant
Caroline Olivier
Jean Pignal
Richard Porzuczek
Barbara Riggs
Cindy Sceviour
Bruce Simpson
Diletta Toneatti
Kim Tremblay
Nathalie Turcotte
Gaye Ward

Alberta, Advanced Education and Career Development, Education Branch

Keith Anderson
Bill Wong

Educational Testing Service

Julie Eastland
Irwin Kirsch
Min Wei Wong
Kentaro Yamamoto

Human Resources Development Canada

Applied Research Branch

Doug Giddings

National Literacy Secretariat

Johanne Lussier
James E. Page
Margaret Robinson
Marla Waltman Daschko

New Brunswick, Advanced Education and Labour

Deborah Burns

Ontario, Training and Adjustment Board

John Stanley

Appendix B

Literacy performance on three scales: definitions and results[1]

Irwin S. Kirsch, Educational Testing Service, Princeton, New Jersey, United States

This chapter explains how to read the results of performance on the three literacy scales...

...which have no intrinsic meaning...

...but relate to tasks and the skills needed to perform them.

The chapter defines the scales and levels, gives examples of tasks and gives country results at each level.

The scales were set up by looking at how people actually perform on various tasks...

The performance results for the 1994 International Adult Literacy Survey (IALS) are reported on three scales—prose, document and quantitative—rather than on a single scale. Each scale ranges from 0 to 500. Scale scores have, in turn, been grouped into five empirically determined literacy levels. As illustrated on page 87, each of these levels implies an ability to cope with a particular subset of reading tasks. The balance of this chapter reports the proficiency achieved on each scale by adults in each participating country, and explains how to interpret this data by describing the scales and the kinds of tasks that were used in the test and the literacy levels that have been adopted.

While the literacy scales make it possible to compare the prose, document and quantitative skills of different populations and to study the relationships between literacy skills and various factors, the scale scores by themselves carry little or no meaning. In other words, whereas most people have a practical understanding of what it means when the temperature outside reaches 10°C, it is not intuitively clear what it means when a particular group is at 287 on the prose scale, or 250 on the document scale, or in Level 2 on the quantitative scale.

One way to gain some understanding about what it means to perform at various points along a literacy scale is to identify a set of variables that can be shown to underlie performance on these tasks. Collectively, these variables provide a framework for understanding what is being measured in a particular assessment and what skills and knowledge are being demonstrated by various levels of proficiency.

Toward this end, the chapter begins by describing how the literacy scale scores were defined. A detailed description of the prose, document and quantitative literacy scales is then provided, including a definition of each of the five levels and the percentages of adults in each of the participating countries demonstrating proficiency in each level. Sample tasks are presented to illustrate the types of materials and task demands that characterize the five levels on each scale.

Defining the literacy levels

The item response theory (IRT) scaling procedures that were used in the IALS provide a statistical solution for establishing one or more scales for a set of tasks in which the ordering of difficulty is essentially the same for everyone. First, the difficulty of tasks is ranked on the scale according to how well respondents actually

1. Reprinted from Chapter 2 (pp. 27–53) of the report *Literacy, Economy and Society: Results of the first International Adult Literacy Survey* (Organisation for Economic Co-operation and Development and Statistics Canada 1995).

...and defining proficiency as having an 80% chance of completing a task at a particular level...

...just as a high jumper is proficient at a height that she or he can usually clear.

The tasks on each scale are ordered according to the skills needed to complete them...

...which can be grouped into five levels requiring successively higher orders of skill...

...which will now be described.

perform them. Next, individuals are assigned scores according to how well they do on a variety of tasks at different levels.

The scale point assigned to each task is the point at which individuals with that proficiency score have a given probability of responding correctly. In this survey, an 80% probability of correct response was the criterion used. This means that individuals estimated to have a particular scale score will consistently perform tasks—with an 80% probability—like those at that point on the scale. It also means they will have a greater than 80% chance of performing tasks that are lower than their estimated proficiency on the scale. It does not mean, however, that individuals with low proficiency can never succeed at more difficult tasks—that is, on tasks with difficulty values higher than their proficiencies. They may do so some of the time. Thus, it means that their probability of success is relatively low. In other words, the more difficult the task relative to their proficiency, the lower the likelihood of a correct response.

An analogy might help clarify this point. The relationship between task difficulty and individual proficiency is much like the high jump event in track and field, in which an athlete tries to jump over a bar that is placed at increasing heights. Each high jumper has a height at which he or she is proficient. That is, the jumper can clear the bar at that height with a high probability of success, and can clear the bar at lower heights almost every time. When the bar is higher than the athlete's level of proficiency, however, it is expected that the athlete will be unable to clear the bar consistently.

Once the literacy tasks are placed along each of the scales using the criterion of 80%, it is possible to see how well the interactions among various task characteristics explain the placement of tasks along the scales. Analyses of the interactions between the materials being read and the tasks based on these materials reveal that an ordered set of information-processing skills appears to be called into play to successfully perform the various tasks displayed along each scale (Kirsch and Mosenthal 1993).

To capture this order, each scale is divided into five levels reflecting the empirically determined progression of information-processing skills and strategies:

- Level 1 (0 to 225)
- Level 2 (226 to 275)
- Level 3 (276 to 325)
- Level 4 (326 to 375)
- Level 5 (376 to 500).

It is worth noting that, while some of the tasks were at the low end of a scale and some at the very high end, most had values in the 200-to-400 range. It is also important to recognize that these levels were selected not as a result of any statistical property of the scales, but rather as the result of shifts in the skills and strategies required to succeed on various tasks along the scales, ranging from simple to complex.

The remainder of this report describes each scale in terms of the nature of task demands at each of the five levels, and reports the proportion of respondents proficient at each level in each country. For each scale, sample tasks at each level are presented, and the factors contributing to their difficulty are discussed. The aim of this chapter is to provide meaning to the scales and to facilitate interpretation of the overall results as well as the breakdowns given in the main body of the report.

	Prose	Document	Quantitative
Level 1 (0 to 225)	Most of the tasks at this level require the reader to locate one piece of information in the text that is identical or synonymous to the information given in the directive. If a plausible incorrect answer is present in the text, it tends not to be near the correct information.	Most of the tasks at this level require the reader to locate a piece of information based on a literal match. Distracting information, if present, is typically located away from the correct answer. Some tasks may direct the reader to enter personal information onto a form.	Although no quantitative tasks used in the IALS fall below the score value of 225, experience suggests that such tasks would require the reader to perform a single, relatively simple operation (usually addition) for which either the numbers are already entered onto the given document and the operation is stipulated, or the numbers are provided and the operation does not require the reader to borrow.
Level 2 (226 to 275)	Tasks at this level tend to require the reader to locate one or more pieces of information in the text, but several distractors may be present, or low-level inferences may be required. Tasks at this level also begin to ask readers to integrate two or more pieces of information, or to compare and contrast information.	Document tasks at this level are a bit more varied. While some still require the reader to match on a single feature, more distracting information may be present or the match may require a low-level inference. Some tasks at this level may require the reader to enter information onto a form or to cycle through information in a document.	Tasks in this level typically require readers to perform a single arithmetic operation (frequently addition or subtraction) using numbers that are easily located in the text or document. The operation to be performed may be easily inferred from the wording of the question or the format of the material (for example, a bank deposit form or an order form).
Level 3 (276 to 325)	Tasks at this level tend to direct readers to search texts to match information that requires low-level inferences or that meets specified conditions. Sometimes the reader is required to identify several pieces of information that are located in different sentences or paragraphs rather than in a single sentence. Readers may also be asked to integrate or to compare and contrast information across paragraphs or sections of text.	Tasks at this level appear to be most varied. Some require the reader to make literal or synonymous matches, but usually the matches require the reader to take conditional information into account or to match on multiple features of information. Some tasks at this level require the reader to integrate information from one or more displays of information. Other tasks ask the reader to cycle through a document to provide multiple responses.	Tasks found in this level typically require the reader to perform a single operation. However, the operations become more varied—some multiplication and division tasks are found in this level. Sometimes two or more numbers are needed to solve the problem and the numbers are frequently embedded in more complex displays. While semantic relation terms such as "how many" or "calculate the difference" are often used, some of the tasks require the reader to make higher order inferences to determine the appropriate operation.
Level 4 (326 to 375)	These tasks require readers to perform multiple-feature matching or to provide several responses where the requested information must be identified through text-based inferences. Tasks at this level may also require the reader to integrate or contrast pieces of information, sometimes presented in relatively lengthy texts. Typically, these texts contain more distracting information and the information that is requested is more abstract.	Tasks at this level, like those in the previous levels, ask the reader to match on multiple features of information, to cycle through documents, and to integrate information; frequently however, these tasks require the reader to make higher order inferences to arrive at the correct answer. Sometimes, conditional information is present in the document, which must be taken into account by the reader.	With one exception, the tasks at this level require the reader to perform a single arithmetic operation where typically either the quantities or the operation are not easily determined. That is, for most of the tasks at this level, the question or directive does not provide a semantic relation term such as "how many" or "calculate the difference" to help the reader.
Level 5 (376 to 500)	Some tasks at this level require the reader to search for information in dense text that contains a number of plausible distractors. Some require readers to make high-level inferences or use specialized knowledge.	Tasks at this level require the reader to search through complex displays of information that contain multiple distractors, to make high-level inferences, process conditional information, or use specialized knowledge.	These tasks require readers to perform multiple operations sequentially, and they must disembed the features of the problem from the material provided or rely on background knowledge to determine the quantities or operations needed.

Interpreting the literacy levels

Prose literacy

Prose literacy is measured using various types of textual material...

The ability to understand and use information contained in various kinds of textual material is an important aspect of literacy. The International Adult Literacy Survey therefore included an array of prose selections, including text from newspapers, magazines and brochures. The material varied in length, density, content, and use of structural or organizational aids such as headings, bullets and special typefaces. All prose samples were reprinted in their entirety with the original layout and typography intact.

...and asking the reader to perform tasks requiring information-processing skills...

Each prose selection was accompanied by one or more questions or directives asking the reader to perform specific tasks. These tasks represent three major aspects of information-processing: *locating*, *integrating* and *generating*. Locating tasks require the reader to find information in the text based on conditions or features specified in the question or directive. The match may be literal or synonymous, or the reader may need to make an inference in order to perform successfully. Integrating tasks ask the reader to pull together two or more pieces of information in the text. In some cases the information can be found in a single paragraph, while in others it appears in different paragraphs or sections. In the generating tasks, readers must produce a written response by processing information from the text and also by making text-based inferences or drawing on their own background knowledge.

...with 34 tasks of varying difficulty being included in the IALS.

In all, the prose literacy scale includes 34 tasks with difficulty values ranging from 188 to 377. These tasks are distributed by level as follows: Level 1 (5 tasks); Level 2 (9 tasks); Level 3 (14 tasks); Level 4 (5 tasks); and Level 5 (1 task). It is important to remember that the tasks requiring the reader to locate, integrate and generate information extend over a range of difficulty as a result of interactions with other variables including:

- the number of categories or features of information the reader must process
- the extent to which information given in the question or directive is obviously related to the information contained in the text
- the amount and location of information in the text that shares some of the features with the information being requested and thus, seems plausible but does not fully answer the question; these are called "distractors"
- the length and density of the text.

The five levels of prose literacy are defined on the following pages.

Percentage of adults by country performing at Level 1:

Canada	16.6
Germany	14.4
Netherlands	10.5
Poland	42.6
Sweden	7.5
Switzerland (French)	17.6
Switzerland (German)	19.3
United States	20.7

Prose Level 1   **Score range: 0 to 225**

Most of the tasks at this level require the reader to locate one piece of information in the text that is identical or synonymous to the information given in the directive. If a plausible incorrect answer is present in the text, it tends not to be near the correct information.

Tasks at this level require the reader to locate and match a single piece of information in the text. Typically the match between the task and the text is literal, although sometimes a low-level inference may be necessary. The text is usually brief or has organizational aids such as paragraph headings or italics that suggest where in the text the reader should search for the specified information. Generally, the target word or phrase appears only once in the text.

The easiest task in Level 1 (difficulty value of 188) directs respondents to look at a medicine label to determine the "maximum number of days you should take this medicine." The label contains only one reference to number of days and this information is located under the heading "DOSAGE." The reader must go to this part of the label and locate the phrase "not longer than 7 days."

MEDCO ASPIRIN *500*

INDICATIONS: Headaches, muscle pains, rheumatic pains, toothaches, earaches. RELIEVES COMMON COLD SYMPTOMS.

DOSAGE: ORAL. 1 or 2 tablets every 6 hours, preferably accompanied by food, for not longer than 7 days. Store in a cool, dry place.

CAUTION: Do not use for gastritis or peptic ulcer. Do not use if taking anticoagulant drugs. Do not use for serious liver illness or bronchial asthma. If taken in large doses and for an extended period, may cause harm to kidneys. Before using this medication for chicken pox or influenza in children, consult with a doctor about Reyes Syndrome, a rare but serious illness. During lactation and pregnancy, consult with a doctor before using this product, especially in the last trimester of pregnancy. If symptoms persist, or in case of an accidental overdose, consult a doctor. Keep out of reach of children.

INGREDIENTS: Each tablet contains 500 mg acetylsalicicylic acid.
Excipient c.b.p.   1 tablet.
Reg. No. 88246

Made in Canada by STERLING PRODUCTS, INC.
1600 Industrial Blvd., Montreal, Quebec H9J 3P1

0 67736 11079

Reprinted by permission

Percentage of adults by country performing at Level 2:

Canada	25.6
Germany	34.2
Netherlands	30.1
Poland	34.5
Sweden	20.3
Switzerland (French)	33.7
Switzerland (German)	35.7
United States	25.9

Prose Level 2   **Score range: 226 to 275**

Tasks at this level tend to require the reader to locate one or more pieces of information in the text, but several distractors may be present, or low-level inferences may be required. Tasks at this level also begin to ask readers to integrate two or more pieces of information, or to compare and contrast information.

Like the tasks at Level 1, most of the tasks at Level 2 ask the reader to locate information. However, more varied demands are placed on the reader in terms of the number of responses the question requires, or in terms of the distracting information that may be present. For example, a task based on an article about the impatiens plant asks the reader to determine what happens when the plant is exposed to temperatures of 14°C or lower. A sentence under the section "**General care**" states that "When the plant is exposed to temperatures of 12-14°C, it loses its leaves and won't bloom anymore." This task received a difficulty value of 230, just in the Level 2 range. What made this task somewhat harder than those identified at Level 1 is that the previous sentence in the text contains information about the requirements of the impatiens plant in various temperatures. This information could have distracted some readers, making the task slightly more difficult.

IMPATIENS

Like many other cultured plants, impatiens plants have a long history behind them. One of the older varieties was sure to be found on grandmother's windowsill. Nowadays, the hybrids are used in many ways in the house and garden.

Origin: The ancestors of the impatiens, *Impatiens sultani* and *Impatiens holstii*, are probably still to be found in the mountain forests of tropical East Africa and on the islands off the coast, mainly Zanzibar. The cultivated European plant received the name *Impatiens walleriana*.

Appearance: It is a herbaceous bushy plant with a height of 30 to 40 cm. The thick, fleshy stems are branched and very juicy, which means, because of the tropical origin, that the plant is sensitive to cold. The light green or white speckled leaves are pointed, elliptical, and slightly indented on the edges. The smooth leaf surfaces and the stems indicate a great need of water.

Bloom: The flowers, which come in all shades of red, appear plentifully all year long, except for the darkest months. They grow from "suckers" (in the stem's "armpit").

Assortment: Some are compact and low-growing types, about 20 to 25 cm. high, suitable for growing in pots. A variety of hybrids can be grown in pots, window boxes, or flower beds. Older varieties with taller stems add dramatic colour to flower beds.

General care: In summer, a place in the shade without direct sunlight is best; in fall and spring, half-shade is best. When placed in a bright spot during winter, the plant requires temperatures of at least 20°C; in a darker spot, a temperature of 15°C will do. When the plant is exposed to temperatures of 12-14°C, it loses its leaves and won't bloom anymore. In wet ground, the stems will rot.

Watering: The warmer and lighter the plant's location, the more water it needs. Always use water without a lot of minerals. It is not known for sure whether or not the plant needs humid air. In any case, do not spray water directly onto the leaves, which causes stains.

Feeding: Feed weekly during the growing period from March to September.

Repotting: If necessary, repot in the spring or in the summer in light soil with humus (prepacked potting soil). It is better to throw the old plants away and start cultivating new ones.

Propagating: Slip or use seeds. Seeds will germinate in ten days.

Diseases: In summer, too much sun makes the plant woody. If the air is too dry, small white flies or aphids may appear.

A similar task involving the same text asks the reader to identify "what the smooth leaf and stem suggest about the plant." The second paragraph of the article is labelled "**Appearance**" and contains a sentence that states, ". . . stems are branched and very juicy, which means, because of the tropical origin, that the plant is sensitive to cold." This sentence distracted some readers from the last sentence in the paragraph: "The smooth leaf surfaces and the stems indicate a great need of water." This task received a difficulty value of 254, placing it in the middle of Level 2.

Percentage of adults by country performing at Level 3:

Canada	35.1
Germany	38.0
Netherlands	44.1
Poland	19.8
Sweden	39.7
Switzerland (French)	38.6
Switzerland (German)	36.1
United States	32.4

Prose Level 3   **Score range: 276 to 325**

Tasks at this level tend to direct readers to search texts to match information that require low-level inferences or that meet specified conditions. Sometimes the reader is required to identify several pieces of information that are located in different sentences or paragraphs rather than in a single sentence. Readers may also be asked to integrate or to compare and contrast information across paragraphs or sections of text.

Tasks at Level 3 on the prose scale tend to require the reader to search for information that requires low-level inferences or that meets conditions stated in the question. Sometimes the reader needs to identify several pieces of information that are located in different sentences or paragraphs rather than in a single sentence. Readers may also be asked to integrate or to compare and contrast information across paragraphs or sections of text.

A task at this level (with a difficulty value of 281) refers the reader to a page from a bicycle owner's manual to determine how to check to make sure the seat is in the proper position. The reader must locate the section labelled "**Fitting the Bicycle**." Then readers must identify and summarize the correct information in writing, making sure the conditions stated are contained in their summary.

PROPER FRAME FIT

RIDER MUST BE ABLE TO STRADDLE BICYCLE WITH AT LEAST 2 cm CLEARANCE ABOVE THE HORIZONTAL BAR WHEN STANDING.

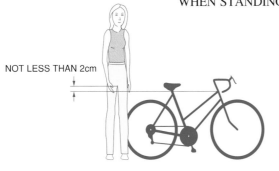

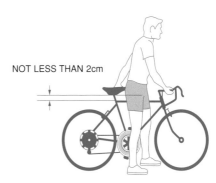

NOT LESS THAN 2cm

NOT LESS THAN 2cm

NOTE: Measurement for a female should be determined using a men's model as a basis.

PROPER SIZE OF BICYCLE	
FRAME SIZE	LEG LENGTH OF RIDER
430mm	660mm-760mm
460mm	690mm-790mm
480mm	710mm-790mm
530mm	760mm-840mm
560mm	790mm-860mm
580mm	810mm-890mm
635mm	860mm-940mm

OWNER'S RESPONSIBILITY

1. **Bicycle Selection and Purchase:** Make sure this bicycle fits the intended rider. Bicycles come in a variety of sizes. Personal adjustment of seat and handlebars is necessary to assure maximum safety and comfort. Bicycles come with a wide variety of equipment and accessories . . . make sure the rider can operate them.

2. **Assembly:** Carefully follow all assembly instructions. Make sure that all nuts, bolts and screws are securely tightened.

3. **Fitting the Bicycle:** To ride safely and comfortably, the bicycle must fit the rider. Check the seat position, adjusting it up or down so that with the sole of rider's foot on the pedal in its lowest position the rider's knee is slightly bent.

Note: Specific charts illustrated at left detail the proper method of deter-mining the correct frame size.

The manufacturer is not responsible for failure, injury, or damage caused by improper completion of assembly or improper maintenance after shipment.

A second Level 3 task, receiving a difficulty value of 310, directs the reader to look at a set of four movie reviews to determine which review was least favourable. Unlike some reviews that rate movies by points or some graphic such as stars, these reviews contain no such indicators. The reader needs to glance at the text of each review to compare what the reviewer said in order to judge which movie received the worst rating.

Another Level 3 question involved an article about cotton diapers. Here readers were asked to write three reasons why the author prefers to use cotton diapers over disposable diapers. This task was relatively difficult (318) because of several variables. First, the reader has to provide several answers requiring text-based inferences. Nowhere in the text does the author say, "I prefer cotton diapers because . . . ." These inferences are made somewhat more difficult because the type of information being requested is a "reason" rather than something more concrete such as a date or person. And finally, the text contains information that may distract the reader.

Percentage of adults by country performing at Level 4:	
Canada	20.0
Germany	12.3
Netherlands	14.6
Poland	2.9
Sweden	26.1
Switzerland (French)	9.5
Switzerland (German)	8.7
United States	17.3

Prose Level 4	Score range: 326 to 375
These tasks require readers to perform multiple-feature matching or to provide several responses where the requested information must be identified through text-based inferences. Tasks at this level may also require the reader to integrate or contrast pieces of information, sometimes presented in relatively lengthy texts. Typically, these texts contain more distracting information and the information that is requested is more abstract.	

One task falling in the middle of Level 4 with a difficulty value of 338 directs readers to use the information from a pamphlet about a hiring interview to "write in your own words one difference between the panel interview and the group interview." Here readers needed to read the brief descriptions about each type of interview. And, rather than merely locating a fact about each or identifying a similarity, they need to integrate what was being presented to infer a characteristic on which the two types of interviews differ. Experience from other large-scale assessments reveals that tasks in which readers are asked to contrast information are more difficult, on average, than tasks in which they are asked to compare information to find similarities.

The Hiring Interview

Preinterview

Try to learn more about the business. What products does it manufacture or services does it provide? What methods or procedures does it use? This information can be found in trade directories, chamber of commerce or industrial directories, or at your local employment office.

Find out more about the position. Would you replace someone or is the position newly created? In which departments or shops would you work? Collective agreements describing various standardized positions and duties are available at most local employment offices. You can also contact the appropriate trade union.

The Interview

Ask questions about the position and the business. Answer clearly and accurately all questions put to you. Bring along a note pad as well as your work and training documents.

The Most Common Types of Interview

One-on-one: Self explanatory.
Panel: A number of people ask you questions and then compare notes on your application.
Group: After hearing a presentation with other applicants on the position and duties, you take part in a group discussion.

Postinterview

Note the key points discussed. Compare questions that caused you difficulty with those that allowed you to highlight your strong points. Such a review will help you prepare for future interviews. If you wish, you can talk about it with the placement officer or career counsellor at your local employment office.

Percentage of adults by country performing at Level 5:	
Canada	2.7
Germany	1.1
Netherlands	0.7
Poland	0.1
Sweden	6.4
Switzerland (French)	0.5
Switzerland (German)	0.3
United States	3.8

Document literacy refers to success in processing everyday documents...

...with 34 tasks of varying difficulty being included in the IALS...

Prose Level 5	Score range: 376 to 500

Some tasks at this level require the reader to search for information in dense text that contains a number of plausible distractors. Some require readers to make high-level inferences or use specialized knowledge.

Two tasks used in this assessment fell in Level 5. One of these tasks, receiving a difficulty value of 377, requires the reader to look at an announcement from a personnel department and "list two ways in which CIEM helps people who will lose their jobs because of a departmental reorganization." The correct response requires readers to search through this text to locate the embedded sentence "CIEM acts as a mediator for employees who are threatened with dismissal resulting from reorganization, and assists with finding new positions when necessary." This task is difficult because the announcement is organized around information that is different from what is being requested in the question. Thus, while the correct information is located in a single sentence, this information is embedded under a list of headings describing CIEM's activities for employees looking for other work. This list of headings serves as an excellent set of distractors for the reader who does not search for or locate the phrase containing the conditional information stated in the directive; that is, those who lose their jobs because of a departmental reorganization.

Document literacy

Adults often encounter materials such as tables, schedules, charts, graphs, maps and forms at home, at work, or when travelling in their communities. The knowledge and skills needed to process information contained in these documents is therefore an important aspect of being literate in a modern society. Success in processing documents appears to depend at least in part on the ability to locate information in a variety of displays, and to use this information in various ways. Sometimes procedural knowledge may be required to transfer information from one source to another, as is necessary in completing applications or order forms.

The IALS document literacy scale contains 34 tasks that are ordered along the scale from 182 to 408 as the result of responses of adults from each of the participating countries. These tasks are distributed as follows: Level 1 (6 tasks); Level 2 (12 tasks); Level 3 (14 tasks); Level 4 (1 task); and Level 5 (1 task). By examining tasks associated with these proficiency levels, characteristics that are likely to make particular document tasks more or less difficult can be identified. Questions or directives associated with the various document tasks are basically of four types: *locating, cycling, integrating* and *generating*. Locating tasks require the reader to match one or more features of information stated in the question to either identical or synonymous information given in the document. Cycling tasks require the reader to locate and match one or more features of information, but differ from locating tasks because they require the reader to engage in a series of feature matches to satisfy conditions given in the question. The integrating tasks typically require the reader to compare and contrast information in adjacent parts of the document. In the generating tasks, readers must produce a written response by processing information found in the document and by making text-based inferences or drawing on their own background knowledge.

CANCO Manufacturing Company
Personnel Department

CANCO

Centre on Internal and External Mobility

What is CIEM?

CIEM stands for Centre on Internal and External Mobility, an initiative of the personnel department. A number of workers of this department work in CIEM, together with members from other departments and outside career consultants.

CIEM is available to help employees in their search for another job inside or outside the Canco Manufacturing Company.

What does CIEM do?

CIEM supports employees who are seriously considering other work through the following activities:
- *Job Data Bank*
After an interview with the employee, information is entered into a data bank that tracks job seekers and job openings at Canco and at other manufacturing companies.
- *Guidance*
The employee's potential is explored through career counselling discussions.
- *Courses*
Courses are being organized (in collaboration with the department for information and training) that will deal with job search and career planning.
- *Career Change Projects*
CIEM supports and coordinates projects to help employees prepare for new careers and new perspectives.
- *Mediation*
CIEM acts as a mediator for employees who are threatened with dismissal resulting from reorganization, and assists with finding new positions when necessary.

How much does CIEM cost?

Payment is determined in consultation with the department where you work. A number of services of CIEM are free. You may also be asked to pay, either in money or in time.

How does CIEM work?

CIEM assists employees who are seriously considering another job within or outside the company.

That process begins by submitting an application. A discussion with a personnel counsellor can also be useful. It is obvious that you should talk with the counsellor first about your wishes and the internal possibilities regarding your career. The counsellor is familiar with your abilities and with developments within your unit.

Contact with CIEM in any case is made via the personnel counsellor. He or she handles the application for you, after which you are invited to a discussion with a CIEM representative.

For more information

The personnel department can give you more information.

...each of which had elements ranging in difficulty.

Here are some examples, together with country results, at each of the five levels.

Percentage of adults by country performing at Level 1:

Canada	18.2
Germany	9.0
Netherlands	10.1
Poland	45.4
Sweden	6.2
Switzerland (French)	16.2
Switzerland (German)	18.1
United States	23.7

As with the prose tasks, each type of question or directive associated with a document task extends over a range of difficulty as a result of interactions among several other characteristics:

- the number of categories or features of information in the question the reader must process or match

- the number of categories or features of information in the document that seem plausible or correct because they share some but not all of the information with the correct answer

- the extent to which the information asked for in the question is obviously related to the information stated in the document

- the structure and content of the document.

A more detailed discussion of the five levels of document literacy follows.

Document Level 1 Score range: 0 to 225

Most of the tasks at this level require the reader to locate a piece of information based on a literal match. Distracting information, if present, is typically located away from the correct answer. Some tasks may direct the reader to enter personal information onto a form.

Tasks at this level require the reader to make a literal match on the basis of a single piece of information. Information that could distract the reader, if present, is typically located away from the correct answer. One document task meeting this description (188) directs the reader to identify from a chart the percentage of teachers from Greece who are women. The chart displays the percentages of women teachers from various countries. Only one number appears on the chart for each country.

FEW DUTCH WOMEN AT THE BLACKBOARD

There is a low percentage of women teachers in the Netherlands compared to other countries. In most of the other countries, the majority of teachers are women. However, if we include the figures for inspectors and school principals, the proportion shrinks considerably and women are in a minority everywhere.

| 74.8 | 72.0 | 63.1 | 61.6 | 58.8 | 58.5 | 57.4 | 51.2 | 41.2 | 38.1 |
| Luxembourg | Italy | France | Ireland | United Kingdom | Spain | Belgium | Greece | Denmark | Netherlands |

Percentage of women teachers (kindergarten, elementary, and secondary).

A very similar task involves a chart displayed in a newspaper showing the expected amounts of radioactive waste by country. This task, which has a difficulty value of 218, directs the reader to identify the country that is projected to have the smallest amount of waste by the year 2000. Again, there is only one percentage associated with each country. In this task, however, the reader must first identify the percentage associated with the smallest amount of waste and then match it to the country.

Percentage of adults by country performing at Level 2:

Canada	24.7
Germany	32.7
Netherlands	25.7
Poland	30.7
Sweden	18.9
Switzerland (French)	28.8
Switzerland (German)	29.1
United States	25.9

Document Level 2   **Score range: 226 to 275**

Document tasks at this level are a bit more varied. While some still require the reader to match on a single feature, more distracting information may be present or the match may require a low-level inference. Some tasks at this level may require the reader to enter information onto a form or to cycle through information in a document.

One Level 2 task on the document scale (242) seems very similar to one described above for Level 1. This task directs the reader to use a chart to identify the year in which the fewest people in the Netherlands were injured by fireworks. Part of what may have made this task somewhat more difficult is that two charts were presented instead of just one. One, labelled "Fireworks in the Netherlands," depicts years and numbers representing funds spent in millions of U.S. dollars, while the other, "Victims of fireworks," uses a line to show numbers of people treated in hospitals. Another contributing factor may have been that neither graph contains the label "number injured by fireworks." The reader needs to make a low inference that victims or number treated equates to injuries.

Several other tasks falling within Level 2 direct the reader to use information given to complete a form. In one case they are asked to fill out an order form to purchase tickets to see a play on a particular day, at a particular time. In another, readers are asked to complete the availability section of an employment application based on information provided that included: total number of hours they are willing to work, hours they are available, how they heard about the job, and availability of transportation.

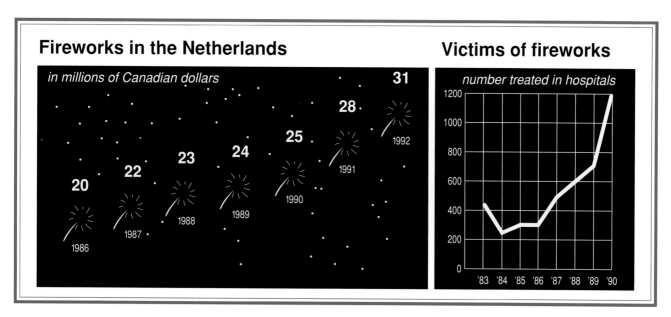

Percentage of adults by country performing at Level 3:	
Canada	32.1
Germany	39.5
Netherlands	44.2
Poland	18.0
Sweden	39.4
Switzerland (French)	38.9
Switzerland (German)	36.6
United States	31.4

Document Level 3   **Score range: 276 to 325**

Tasks at this level appear to be most varied. Some require the reader to make literal or synonymous matches, but usually the matches require the reader to take conditional information into account or to match on multiple features of information. Some tasks at this level require the reader to integrate information from one or more displays of information. Other tasks ask the reader to cycle through a document to provide multiple responses.

One task falling around the middle of Level 3 in difficulty involves the fireworks charts shown earlier (see page 97). This task directs the reader to write a brief description of the relationship between sales and injuries based on the information shown in the two graphs. This task received a difficulty value of 295. A second task, receiving a similar difficulty value, directs readers to a bus schedule. They are asked to identify the time of the last bus they could take from a particular location on a Saturday night. Here the reader must match several pieces of information—the last time, a particular location, on Saturday, in the evening—to arrive at a correct answer. This task received a difficulty value of 297.

QUICK COPY Printing Requisition

FILL IN ALL INFORMATION REQUESTED

GUIDELINES: This requisition may be used to order materials to be printed BLACK INK only, and in the quantities that are listed at the right.

■ SINGLE SHEET PRINTED 1 OR 2 SIDES — 2000 copies maximum
■ MORE THAN ONE SHEET UP TO 100 PAGES — 400 copies maximum
                        OVER 100 PAGES — 200 copies maximum

1. PROJECT TO BE CHARGED

2. TODAY'S DATE

3. TITLE OR DESCRIPTION

4. DATE DELIVERY REQUIRED

5. DO NOT MARK IN SHADED BOXES

NUMBER OF ORIGINALS X NUMBER OF COPIES TO BE PRINTED = TOTAL NUMBER OF IMPRESSIONS

6. NUMBER OF SIDES TO BE PRINTED (Check one box.)   1 ☐ One side   2 ☐ BOTH sides

7. COLOR OF PAPER (Fill in only if NOT white.) _____

8. SIZE OF PAPER (Fill in only if NOT 8½ x 11) _____

9. Check any that apply:
   ☐ COLLATE
   BINDING: ☐ One staple at upper left
            ☐ Two staples in left margin
            ☐ BIND-FAST: ☐ Black
                         ☐ Brown
            ☐ 3-hole punch
   ☐ Other instructions _____

AUTHORIZATION AND DELIVERY

10. Project Director (print name) _____

11. Requisitioner (print your own name and phone no.) _____
    extension

12. Check one:
    ☐ Requisitioner will PICK UP completed job.
    ☐ Mail completed job to: _____
       Print name, room number, and mail stop

    MAIL STOP

    ROOM NO.

13. **KEEP PINK COPY at least 3 months.** When requesting information, you must refer to the requisition number printed here.

140468

QUICK COPY REGISTRATION NUMBER

D1320-03116 • 000000 • 000000

A third task, falling at high end of Level 3 (321), involves the use of a quick copy printing requisition form that might be found in the workplace. The task asks the reader to explain whether or not the quick copy centre would make 300 copies of a statement that is 105 pages long. In responding to this directive, the reader must determine whether conditions stated in the question meet those provided in the guidelines to this document.

Percentage of adults by country performing at Level 4:

Canada	19.6
Germany	17.0
Netherlands	18.5
Poland	5.5
Sweden	27.8
Switzerland (French)	14.2
Switzerland (German)	14.2
United States	15.3

Document Level 4 Score range: 326 to 375

Tasks at this level, like those in the previous levels, ask the reader to match on multiple features of information, to cycle through documents, and to integrate information; frequently however, these tasks require the reader to make higher order inferences to arrive at the correct answer. Sometimes, conditional information is present in the document, which must be taken into account by the reader.

The only task falling at this level (341) asks the reader to look at two pie charts showing oil use for 1970 and 1989. The question directs the reader to summarize how the percentages of oil used for different purposes changed over the period specified. Here the reader must cycle through the two charts, comparing and contrasting the percentages for each of the four stated purposes. Then the reader must generate a statement that captures these changes.

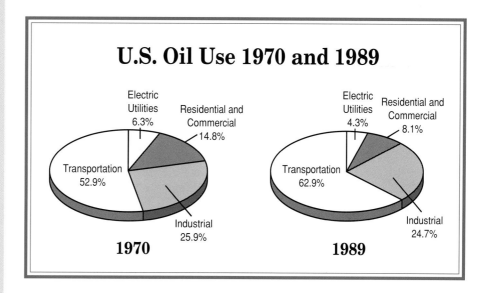

Percentage of adults by country performing at Level 5:

Canada	5.4
Germany	1.9
Netherlands	1.4
Poland	0.4
Sweden	7.7
Switzerland (French)	1.9
Switzerland (German)	1.9
United States	3.7

Document Level 5 Score range: 376 to 500

Tasks at this level require the reader to search through complex displays of information that contain multiple distractors, to make high-level inferences, process conditional information, or use specialized knowledge.

The only Level 5 task in this international assessment involved a page taken from a consumer magazine rating clock radios. The most difficult task (408) involving this document asked the reader for the average advertised price for the basic clock radio receiving the highest overall score. As can be seen on page 101, this task required readers to process two types of conditional information. First, they needed to identify the radio receiving the highest overall score while distinguishing among the three types of clock radios reviewed: full-featured, basic and those with a cassette player. Second, they needed to locate a price. In making this final match, they needed to notice that two prices were given; the first, the suggested retail and the second, the average advertised price.

A second and considerably easier task involving this document and falling at the high end of Level 2 (321) asks the reader "which full-featured radio is rated the highest on performance." Again, readers needed to find the correct category of clock radio. Yet, they needed to process fewer conditions. Here they only needed to distinguish between the rating for "Overall Score" and "Performance." It is possible that some adults identified the full-featured radio as receiving the highest "Overall Score" rather than the one rated highest in "Performance" as specified in the question. As such, "Overall Score" would be considered a plausible distractor. Another factor that likely contributed to this task's difficulty is that "Overall Score" is given a numerical value while the other features are rated by a symbol. It may be that some adults found the correct category ("Performance"), but selected the first radio listed, assuming it performed best. The text accompanying this table indicates the radios are rated within a category by overall score. It is easy to imagine that some people may have equated overall score with overall performance.

Quantitative literacy

Quantitative literacy also requires the processing of printed information...

Since adults are frequently required to perform arithmetic operations in everyday life, the ability to perform quantitative literacy tasks is another important aspect of literacy. These skills may seem, at first glance, to be fundamentally different from the types of knowledge and skill associated with prose and document literacy and therefore, to extend the concept of literacy beyond its traditional limits. However, experience in North America with large-scale assessments of adults indicates that the processing of printed information plays an important role in affecting the difficulty of tasks along the scale (Kirsch et al. 1993; Montigny et al. 1991).

...which makes arithmetic skills inadequate on their own.

In general, it appears that many individuals can perform single arithmetic operations when both the numbers and operations are made explicit. However, when the numbers to be used must be located in and extracted from different types of documents that contain similar but irrelevant information, when the operations to be used must be inferred from printed directions, and when multiple operations must be performed, the tasks become increasingly difficult.

There were 33 quantitative literacy tasks in the IALS...

The IALS quantitative literacy scale contains 33 tasks ranging from 225 to 408 in difficulty. These tasks are distributed as follows: Level 1 (1 task); Level 2 (9 tasks); Level 3 (15 tasks); Level 4 (6 tasks); and Level 5 (2 tasks). The difficulty of these tasks and, therefore, their placement along the scale, appears to be a function of several factors including:

- the particular arithmetic operation required to complete the task
- the number of operations needed to perform the task successfully
- the extent to which the numbers are embedded in printed materials
- the extent to which an inference must be made to identify the type of operation to be performed.

RATINGS

Better ◐ ◑ ○ ◒ ● Worse

Clock radios

Listed by types; within types, listed in order of overall score. Differences in score of 4 points or less were not deemed significant.

1 Brand and model. If you can't find a model, call the company. Phone numbers are listed on page 736.

2 Price. The manufacturer's suggested or approximate retail price, followed by the average advertised price.

3 Dimensions. To the nearest centimetre.

4 Overall score. A composite, encompassing all our tests and judgments. A "perfect" radio would have earned 100 points.

5 Convenience. This composite judgment reflects such things as the legibility of the display, the ease of tuning the radio and setting the alarm, and the presence or absence of useful features.

6 Performance. An overall judgment reflecting performance in our tests of: sensitivity and selectivity; tuning ease; capture ratio, the ability to bring in the stronger of two stations on the same frequency; image rejection, the ability to ignore signals from just above the band, resistance to interference from signals bouncing off aircraft and such.

7 Sensitivity. How well each radio received a station with little interference.

8 Selectivity. How well each radio received clearly a weak station next to a strong one on the dial.

9 Tone quality. Based mainly on computer analysis of the speaker's output and on listening tests, using music from CDs. No model produced high-fidelity sound.

10 Reversible time-setting. This useful feature makes setting clock and alarm times easy. If you overshoot the desired setting, you simply back up.

11 Dual alarm. Lets you set two separate wake-up times.

Brand and model	Price	Dimensions, HxWxD, cm.	Overall Score	Convenience	Performance	Sensitivity	Selectivity	Tone quality	Reversible time-setting	Dual alarm	Warranty, months	Advantages	Disadvantages	Comments
Full-featured clock radios														
RCA RP-3690	$50/$40	8x25x18	86	◐	◑	◑	◑	◐	✔	✔	12	A,B,D,H,J,L,O,T,U		A
Sony ICF-C303	50/45	5x20x15	84	◐	◑	◐	○	◑	✔	✔	12	C,E,F,I,N,T		C
Panasonic RC-X220	50/45	10x28x13	82	◑	◑	◑	◑	○	✔	✔	12	A,G,K,M,O,S,T,U	b,c	A
Realistic 272	50/30	5x28x15	79	◑	○	◑	◑	◑	✔	✔	3	A,G,H,K,O,T		D
Magnavox AJ3900	65/—	15x38x13	78	○	◐	◑	◐	◑	—	✔	3	D,G,K,M,O,R,T	b,g	B
Emerson AK2745	39/20	8x28x15	70	○	◑	◑	◑	○	✔	✔	3	G,O	g	K
Soundesign 3753	20/20	8x23x13	62	○	◑	●	○	○	✔	✔	3	J,Q	d,h	J
Basic clock radios														
Realistic 263	28/18	10x20x10	74	○	◑	◑	○	◑	—	—	3	A,D,H,O,P,U	h	—
Soundesign 3622	12/10	5x20x13	68	◑	◑	◐	○	◑	—	—	3	U	d	L
Panasonic RC-6064	18/15	5x20x13	67	◑	◑	◐	○	◑	—	—	12	—	b,c	—
General Electric 7-4612	13/10	5x20x13	66	◑	○	◐	◑	○	—	—	12	A,D	a,g	—
Lloyds CR001	20/15	5x18x13	64	◑	○	◐	○	◑	—	—	3	U	—	—
Sony ICF-C240	15/13	5x18x15	63	◑	○	◑	○	◑	—	—	12	—	f,g	—
Emerson AK2720	19/10	5x20x13	61	◑	○	◑	●	○	—	—	3	O,T	e	K
Gran Prix D507	15/10	5x18x10	54	◑	●	○	●	●	—	—	3	—	d	—
Clock radios with cassette player														
General Electric 7-4965	60/50	10x30x15	85	◑	◑	◑	◑	◑	✔	✔	12	A,D,G,H,K,O,S,T	—	B,E
Pansonic RC-X250	[1]	10x33x13	76	◑	◑	○	◑	◑	✔	✔	12	A,G,K,O,R,U	b,c	A,H
Sony ICF-CS650	75/65	15x28x15	74	○	◑	◐	○	◑	✔	✔	12	G,R,T,U	c,f,i	A,F,H
Soundesign 3844MGY	40/30	13x30x13	62	○	●	◐	●	◑	—	—	3	G,K,J,S,U		F,G,I,M

[1] *Discontinued. Replaced by* **RC-X260**, *$79 list and $60 average advertised sale price.*

Features in Common

All: • Permit snooze time of about 8 min. • Retain time settings during short power failures.
Except as noted, all have: • Battery backup for clock and alarm memory. • Red display digits 1 cm. high. • Sleep-time radio play for up to 60 min. before automatic shutoff. • Switch to reset alarm.

Keys to Advantages

A–Alarm works despite power failure.
B–Shows actual time plus up to 2 alarm times.
C–Twin alarms settable for 2 different stations.
D–Tone alarm has adjustable volume control.
E–Memory needs no battery.
F–Digital tuner with presettable stations.
G–Tuner can receive in stereo.
H–Battery-strength indicator.
I–Illuminated tuning dial.
J–Illuminated tuning pointer.
K–Earphone jack.
L–Nap timer.
M–Audio input for tape deck or CD player.
N–Display can show date and time.
O–Display has high/low brightness switch.
P–Display has larger digits than most.
Q–Night light—adjusts for room light.
R–Bass-boost tone control.
S–Treble-cut tone control.
T–Better than most in tuning ease.
U–Better than most in image rejection.

Key to Disadvantages

a–Possible to reset time by accident.
b–Controls for time-setting or dimmer inconveniently located on radio's bottom or rear.
c–Display dimmer than most in brightly lit room.
d–Radio volume must be turned completely down for alarm buzzer to sound.
e–Lacks alarm buzzer; radio is sole alarm.
f–Lacks indication alarm is set.
g–Lacks alarm-reset button.
h–Time-setting lacks fast reverse.
i–No slow forward, fast reverse for time setting.

Key to Comments

A–Display shows green digits.
B–Display shows blue digits.
C–Display uses LCD (liquid crystal) digits.
D–Terminals for external antenna.
E–3-position graphic equalizer.
F–Cassette player lacks Record function.
G–Cassette player lacks Rewind function.
H–Model permits wake-up to cassette play.
I–Cassette-deck flutter worse than most.
J–Warranty repairs cost $3 for handling.
K–Warranty repairs cost $3.50 for handling.
L–Warranty repairs cost $6 for handling.
M–Warranty repairs cost $10 for handling.

A detailed discussion of the five levels of quantitative literacy follows.

Percentage of adults by country performing at Level 1:

Canada	16.9
Germany	6.7
Netherlands	10.3
Poland	39.1
Sweden	6.6
Switzerland (French)	12.9
Switzerland (German)	14.2
United States	21.0

Quantitative Level 1	Score range: 0 to 225

Although no quantitative tasks used in the IALS fall below the score value of 225, experience suggests that such tasks would require the reader to perform a single, relatively simple operation (usually addition) for which either the numbers are already entered onto the given document and the operation is stipulated, or the numbers are provided and the operation does not require the reader to borrow.

The easiest quantitative task in the IALS (225) directs the reader to complete an order form. The last line on this form says "Total with Handling." The line above it says "Handling Charge $2.00." The reader simply had to add the $2.00 to the $50.00 they had entered on a previous line to indicate the cost of the tickets. In this task, one of the numbers was stipulated, the operation was easily identified from the word "total" and the operation did not require the reader to borrow. Moreover, the format of the form set the problem up in a simple column format, further facilitating the task for the reader.

Percentage of adults by country performing at Level 2:

Canada	26.1
Germany	26.6
Netherlands	25.5
Poland	30.1
Sweden	18.6
Switzerland (French)	24.5
Switzerland (German)	26.2
United States	25.3

Quantitative Level 2	Score range: 226 to 275

Tasks in this level typically require readers to perform a single arithmetic operation (frequently addition or subtraction) using numbers that are easily located in the text or document. The operation to be performed may be easily inferred from the wording of the question or the format of the material (for example, a bank deposit form or an order form).

A typical Level 2 task on the quantitative scale directs the reader to use a weather chart in a newspaper to determine how many degrees warmer today's high temperature is expected to be in Bangkok than in Seoul. Here the reader had to cycle through the table to locate the two temperatures and then subtract them to determine the difference. This task received a difficulty value of 255.

WEATHER

Europe

	Today			Tomorrow		
	High	Low	W	High	Low	W
	C	C		C	C	
Algarve	19	7	s	21	9	s
Amsterdam	11	6	pc	12	7	pc
Ankara	17	7	pc	19	8	pc
Athens	22	15	pc	23	14	pc
Barcelona	16	8	s	14	9	s
Belgrade	14	6	pc	10	1	c
Berlin	8	2	c	6	1	c
Brussels	11	6	pc	14	7	pc
Budapest	9	1	pc	9	2	c
Copenhagen	7	1	r	6	2	c
Costa del Sol	21	8	s	21	10	s
Dublin	10	6	pc	13	8	pc
Edinburgh	10	6	c	10	6	c
Florence	11	5	s	14	6	s
Frankfurt	12	6	pc	13	4	pc
Geneva	9	2	s	12	4	s
Helsinki	-1	-7	sf	-3	-10	pc
Istanbul	17	10	pc	15	9	sh
Las Palmas	26	18	pc	27	18	pc
Lisbon	19	9	s	19	10	s
London	12	5	pc	13	7	pc
Madrid	17	3	s	18	4	s
Milan	9	3	s	13	6	s
Moscow	1	-3	r	-3	-11	sf
Munich	11	3	pc	12	6	pc
Nice	14	7	s	15	8	s
Oslo	4	-4	c	5	-2	c
Paris	12	6	pc	13	6	pc
Prague	11	1	pc	8	2	c
Reykjavik	4	2	r	6	-1	c
Rome	20	12	s	20	10	s
St. Petersburg	-1	-7	sf	-4	-12	pc
Stockholm	1	-5	sn	-2	-7	c
Strasbourg	12	5	pc	15	7	pc
Tallinn	-1	-7	sf	-4	-10	pc
Venice	10	3	s	11	4	s
Vienna	9	-1	pc	10	2	c
Warsaw	8	2	sh	6	1	c
Zurich	8	0	s	9	1	pc

Oceania

Auckland	20	14	s	17	11	sh
Sydney	27	17	pc	25	16	pc

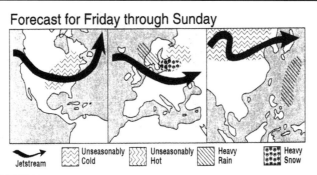

Forecast for Friday through Sunday

Jetstream — Unseasonably Cold — Unseasonably Hot — Heavy Rain — Heavy Snow

North America
Cold weather will engulf the Midwestern and Northeastern United States Friday and over the weekend. Although it will be cold in Chicago, Toronto and New York City, the weather will have some sunshine and seasonable temperatures each day.

Europe
Western and central Europe will have a spell of mild weather Friday into the weekend. London and Paris will have dry weather with some sunshine Friday into Sunday. Rain will continue to soak southwestern Norway. Snow will blanket the area from Minsk to Moscow.

Asia
Typhoon Elsie will probably stay to the east of the Philippines and south of Japan Friday and the weekend. Some rain is apt to fall in Seoul and there could even be a little ice or snow. Cold air will pour into Beijing and snow is a possibility. Hong Kong will start the weekend warm.

Asia

	Today			Tomorrow		
	High	Low	W	High	Low	W
	C	C		C	C	
Bangkok	32	22	pc	30	23	s
Beijing	11	0	s	8	2	pc
Hong Kong	30	23	s	29	22	pc
Manila	31	25	s	31	25	sh
New Delhi	31	13	s	32	16	s
Seoul	14	6	pc	14	4	pc
Shanghai	22	10	pc	24	12	s
Singapore	31	24	pc	28	23	sh
Taipei	26	21	pc	26	19	pc
Tokyo	18	9	pc	17	7	pc

Africa

Algiers	27	14	s	26	13	s
Cape Town	20	11	sh	18	11	pc
Casablanca	20	14	c	21	11	pc
Harare	34	17	s	32	18	pc
Lagos	30	24	pc	29	24	pc
Nairobi	27	12	pc	26	13	pc
Tunis	27	17	pc	17	14	pc

North

Anchorage	0	-2	c	3	0	sh
Atlanta	14	4	pc	8	2	pc
Boston	15	4	c	8	-1	pc
Chicago	2	-5	c	-2	-8	pc
Denver	8	-3	pc	4	-6	sn
Detroit	4	-2	c	4	-5	pc
Honolulu	31	20	s	31	21	pc
Houston	15	3	pc	12	6	pc
Los Angeles	28	14	s	24	13	s
Miami	30	22	pc	29	21	pc
Minneapolis	-1	-8	c	1	-7	pc
Montreal	7	-2	sf	4	-3	c
Nassau	31	22	pc	28	21	sh
New York	14	4	r	10	2	pc
Phoenix	23	11	pc	22	8	s
San Fran.	20	11	pc	21	8	s
Seattle	11	6	pc	13	7	r
Toronto	6	-3	c	3	-3	c
Washington	14	6	r	11	4	pc

Middle East

	Today			Tomorrow		
	High	Low	W	High	Low	w
	C	C		C	C	
Beirut	28	19	pc	29	20	s
Cairo	29	20	pc	28	19	pc
Damascus	24	12	s	26	14	s
Jerusalem	27	15	s	26	14	s
Riyadh	34	13	s	32	13	s

Latin America

	Today			Tomorrow		
	High	Low	W	High	Low	W
	C	C		C	C	
Buenos Aires	23	11	pc	26	13	s
Caracas	29	20	s	31	18	s
Lima	23	17	c	23	16	c
Mexico City	23	11	sh	23	12	pc
Rio de Janiero	32	22	s	28	21	sh
Santiago	24	4	s	22	6	pc

Legend: s-sunny, pc-partly cloudy, c-cloudy, sh-showers, t-thunderstorms, r-rain, sf-snow flurries, sn-snow, i-ice, W-Weather. **All maps, forecasts and data provided by Accu-Weather, Inc.© 1992**

A similar but slightly more difficult task (268) requires the reader to use the chart about women in the teaching profession in Europe that is displayed in Level 1 for the document scale (see page 96). This task directs the reader to calculate the percentage of men in the teaching profession in Italy. Both this task and the one just mentioned involved calculating the difference between two numbers. Part of what distinguishes these two tasks is that in the former, both temperatures could be identified in the table from the newspaper. For the task involving men teachers in Italy, the reader needed to make the inference that the percentage of men teachers is equal to 100% minus the percentage of women teachers.

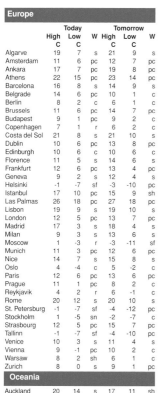

Percentage of adults by country performing at Level 3:

Canada	34.8
Germany	43.2
Netherlands	44.3
Poland	23.9
Sweden	39.0
Switzerland (French)	42.2
Switzerland (German)	40.7
United States	31.3

Quantitative Level 3   **Score range: 276 to 325**

Tasks found in this level typically require the reader to perform a single operation. However, the operations become more varied—some multiplication and division tasks are found in this level. Sometimes two or more numbers are needed to solve the problem and the numbers are frequently embedded in more complex displays. While semantic relation terms such as "how many" or "calculate the difference" are often used, some of the tasks require the reader to make higher order inferences to determine the appropriate operation.

Tasks falling around 300 on the quantitative scale still require the reader to perform single arithmetic operations, but the operations become more varied. Part of what distinguishes tasks at this level from those seen at lower levels is that the displays of information become more complex and the reader must identify two or more numbers from various places in the document. For example, one task located at 302 on the quantitative scale directs the reader to look at two graphs containing information about consumers and producers of primary energy. In one question, they are asked to calculate how much more energy Canada produces than it consumes. Here the operation is not facilitated by the format of the document and the reader must locate the information using both bar graphs. In another question using this document, the reader is directed to calculate the total amount of energy in quadrillion (10^{15}) Btu consumed by Canada, Mexico and the United States. This task falls at 300 on the scale. It requires the reader to add three numbers. Presenting two graphs likely contributed to the difficulty of this task. Some respondents may have performed the appropriate calculation for the three countries specified using the producer energy chart rather than the consumer energy chart.

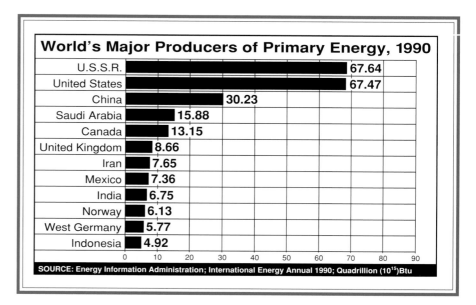

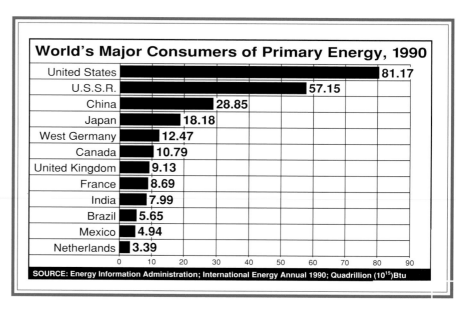

Another task at this level involves the fireworks chart shown earlier for the document scale (see page 97). This quantitative task asks the reader to calculate how many more people were injured in 1989 than in 1988. What contributes to this task receiving a difficulty value of 293 is that one of the numbers was not given in the line graph. The reader needed to interpolate the number from information provided along the vertical axis.

In a more difficult task (located at 317 on the scale), readers are asked to look at a recipe for scrambled eggs with tomatoes. The recipe gives the ingredients for four servings: 3 tablespoons of oil, 1 garlic clove, 1 teaspoon of sugar, 500 grams of fresh red tomatoes and 6 eggs. The question asks them to determine the number of eggs they will need if they are using the recipe for six people. Here they must know how to calculate or determine the ratio needed. This task is somewhat easier than might be expected, given other tasks at this level. This may be because people are familiar with recipes and with manipulating them to fit a particular situation.

This appears to be true for another question using this recipe. It asks the reader to determine the amount of oil that would be needed if the recipe were being used for two people. This task received a value of 253 on the scale. A larger percentage of respondents found it easier to halve an ingredient than to increase one by 50%. It is not clear why this is so. It may be that some of the respondents have an algorithm for responding to certain familiar tasks that does not require them to apply general arithmetic principles for solving the problem.

Percentage of adults by country performing at Level 4:

Canada	17.5
Germany	20.7
Netherlands	17.8
Poland	6.1
Sweden	27.4
Switzerland (French)	19.2
Switzerland (German)	17.1
United States	17.5

Quantitative Level 4   **Score range: 326 to 375**

With one exception, the tasks at this level require the reader to perform a single arithmetic operation where typically either the quantities or the operation are not easily determined. That is, for most of the tasks at this level, the question or directive does not provide a semantic relation term such as "how many" or "calculate the difference" to help the reader.

Tasks around 350 on the quantitative scale tend to require the application of a single operation where either the quantities or the operation are not easily determined. One such task involves a compound interest table. It directs the reader to "calculate the total amount of money you will have if you invest $100 at a rate of 6% for 10 years." This task received a difficulty value of 348, in part because many people treated this as a document rather than a quantitative task and simply looked up the amount of interest that would be earned. They likely forgot to add the interest to their $100 investment.

Compound Interest
Compounded Annually

Principal	Period	4%	5%	6%	7%	8%	9%	10%	12%	14%	16%
$100	1 day	0.011	0.014	0.016	0.019	0.022	0.025	0.027	0.033	0.038	0.044
	1 week	0.077	0.096	0.115	0.134	0.153	0.173	0.192	0.230	0.268	0.307
	6 mos	2.00	2.50	3.00	3.50	4.00	4.50	5.00	6.00	7.00	8.00
	1 year	4.00	5.00	6.00	7.00	8.00	9.00	10.00	12.00	14.00	16.00
	2 years	8.16	10.25	12.36	14.49	16.64	18.81	21.00	25.44	29.96	34.56
	3 years	12.49	15.76	19.10	22.50	25.97	29.50	33.10	40.49	48.15	56.09
	4 years	16.99	21.55	26.25	31.08	36.05	41.16	46.41	57.35	68.90	81.06
	5 years	21.67	27.63	33.82	40.26	46.93	53.86	61.05	76.23	92.54	110.03
	6 years	26.53	34.01	41.85	50.07	58.69	67.71	77.16	97.38	119.50	143.64
	7 years	31.59	40.71	50.36	60.58	71.38	82.80	94.87	121.07	150.23	182.62
	8 years	36.86	47.75	59.38	71.82	85.09	99.26	114.36	147.60	185.26	227.84
	9 years	42.33	55.13	68.95	83.85	99.90	117.19	135.79	177.31	225.19	280.30
	10 years	48.02	62.89	79.08	96.72	115.89	136.74	159.37	210.58	270.72	341.14
	12 years	60.10	79.59	101.22	125.22	151.82	181.27	213.84	289.60	381.79	493.60
	15 years	80.09	107.89	139.66	175.90	217.22	264.25	317.72	447.36	613.79	826.55
	20 years	119.11	165.33	220.71	286.97	366.10	460.44	572.75	864.63	1,274.35	1,846.08

Another task at this level requires respondents to read a newspaper article describing a research finding linking allergies to a particular genetic mutation. The question directs the reader to calculate the number of people studied who were found to have the mutant gene. To answer the question correctly, readers must know how to convert the phrase "64 percent" to a decimal number and then multiply it by the number of patients studied (400). The text provides no clues on how to set up this problem.

A third task involves the distance chart shown on the next page. Readers were asked to "calculate the total number of kilometres travelled in a trip from Guadalajara to Tecoman and then to Zamora." Here a semantic relation term was provided, but the quantities were not easily identified. As a result, this task received a difficulty value of 335. Making the inference that the trip was from Guadalajara to Tecoman and then from Tecoman to Zamora was difficult for some respondents. In a different task, respondents were asked to determine how much less the distance from Guadalajara to Tecoman is than the distance from Guadalajara to Puerto Vallarta. In this Level 3 task (308), the quantities were relatively easy to locate.

TABLE OF APPROXIMATE DISTANCES (in kilometres)

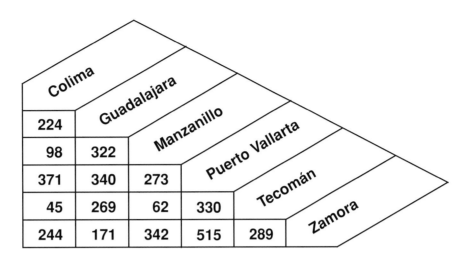

Colima	Guadalajara	Manzanillo	Puerto Vallarta	Tecomán	Zamora
224					
98	322				
371	340	273			
45	269	62	330		
244	171	342	515	289	

Quantitative Level 5	Score range: 376 to 500

These tasks require readers to perform multiple operations sequentially, and they must disembed the features of the problem from the material provided or rely on background knowledge to determine the quantities or operations needed.

One of the most difficult tasks on the quantitative scale (381) requires readers to look at a table providing nutritional analysis of food and then, using the information given, determine the percentage of calories in a Big Mac® that comes from total fat. To answer this question, readers must first recognize that the information about total fat provided is given in grams. In the question, they are told that a gram of fat has 9 calories. Therefore, they must convert the number of fat grams to calories. Then, they need to calculate this number of calories as a percentage of the total calories given for a Big Mac®. Only one other item on this scale received a higher score.

Estimating literacy performance across the levels

The literacy levels not only provide a means for exploring the progression of information-processing demands across each of the scales, but they also can be used to help explain how the proficiencies individuals demonstrate reflect the likelihood they will respond correctly to the broad range of tasks used in this assessment as well as to similar tasks that were not included. In practical terms, this means that individuals performing at 250 on each scale are expected to be able to perform the average Level 1 and 2 tasks with a high degree of proficiency. That is, they will be able to perform these kinds of tasks with an average probability of 80% or higher. It does not mean that they will not be able to perform tasks in Levels 3 or higher. They will do so some of the time, but not consistently.

Nutritional Analysis

	Serving Size	Calories	Protein (g)	Carbohydrates (g)	Total Fat (g)	Saturated Fat (g)	Monounsaturated Fat (g)	Polyunsaturated Fat (g)	Cholesterol (mg)	Sodium (mg)
Sandwiches										
Hamburger	102 g	255	12	30	9	5	1	3	37	490
Cheeseburger	116 g	305	15	30	13	7	1	5	50	725
Quarter Pounder®	166 g	410	23	34	20	11	1	8	85	645
Quarter Pounder® w/Cheese	194 g	510	28	34	28	16	1	11	115	1110
McLean Deluxe™	206 g	320	22	35	10	5	1	4	60	670
McLean Deluxe™ w/Cheese	219 g	370	24	35	14	8	1	5	75	890
Big Mac®	215 g	500	25	42	26	16	1	9	100	890
Filet-O-Fish®	141 g	370	14	38	18	8	6	4	50	730
McChicken®	187 g	415	19	39	19	9	7	4	50	830
French Fries										
Small French Fries	68 g	220	3	26	12	8	1	2.5	0	110
Medium French Fries	97 g	320	4	36	17	12	1.5	3.5	0	150
Large French Fries	122 g	400	6	46	22	15	2	5	0	200
Salads										
Chef Salad	265 g	170	17	8	9	4	1	4	111	400
Garden Salad	189 g	50	4	6	2	1	0.4	0.6	65	70
Chunky Chicken Salad	255 g	150	25	7	4	2	1	1	78	230
Side Salad	106 g	30	2	4	1	0.5	0.2	0.3	33	35
Croutons	11 g	50	1	7	2	1.3	0.1	0.5	0	140
Bacon Bits	3 g	15	1	0	1	0.3	0.2	0.5	1	95

Soft Drinks

	Coca-Cola Classic®				diet Coke®				Sprite®			
	Small	Medium	Large	Jumbo	Small	Medium	Large	Jumbo	Small	Medium	Large	Jumbo
Calories	140	190	260	380	1	1	2	3	140	190	260	380
Carbohydrates (g)	38	50	70	101	0.3	0.4	0.5	0.6	36	48	66	96
Sodium (mg)	15	20	25	40	30	40	60	80	15	20	25	40

These probabilities are shown in Tables 2.1a to 2.1c, and are explained here.

The three charts given in Tables 2.1a to 2.1c display the probability that individuals performing at selected points on each of the scales will give a correct response to tasks of varying difficulty. For example, a reader whose prose proficiency is 150 has less than a 50% chance of giving a correct response to the Level 1 tasks. Individuals whose proficiency score is 200, in contrast, have about an 80% probability of responding correctly to these Level 1 tasks.

In terms of task demands, it can be inferred that adults performing at 200 on the prose scale are likely to be able to locate a single piece of information in a brief text when there is no distracting information, or if plausible but incorrect information is present but located away from the correct answer. However, these individuals are likely to demonstrate far more difficulty with tasks in Levels 2 through 5. For example, they would have only about a 40% chance of performing the average Level 2 task correctly and an 18% chance of success with tasks in Level 3 and no more than a 7% chance with tasks in Levels 4 and 5.

Tables B.1a to B.1c

Average probabilities of successful performance by individuals with selected proficiency scores on tasks in each literacy level of the prose, document and quantitative scales

---

Tables B.1a
Prose scale

Prose level	Selected proficiency scores				
	150	200	250	300	350
			%		
1	48	81	95	99	100
2	14	40	76	94	99
3	6	18	46	78	93
4	2	7	21	50	80
5*	2	6	18	40	68

Document level	Selected proficiency scores				
	150	200	250	300	350

Table B.1b
Document scale

	150	200	250	300	350
			%		
1	40	72	94	99	100
2	19	50	82	95	99
3	7	20	49	79	94
4*	4	12	31	60	83
5*	<1	1	3	13	41

Quantitative level	Selected proficiency scores				
	150	200	250	300	350
			%		

Table B.1c
Quantitative scale

	150	200	250	300	350
1*	34	67	89	97	99
2	20	45	75	92	98
3	7	20	48	78	93
4	1	6	22	58	87
5	1	2	7	20	53

*Probabilities in this row are based on one task.

In contrast, respondents demonstrating a proficiency of 300 on the prose scale have about an 80% chance or higher of succeeding on tasks in Levels 1, 2 and 3. This means that they demonstrate success with tasks that require them to make low-level inferences and with tasks that require them to take some conditional information into account. They can also integrate or compare and contrast information that is easily identified in the text. On the other hand, they are likely to demonstrate some difficulty with tasks where they must make high text-based inferences or where they need to process more abstract types of information. These more difficult tasks may also require them to draw on less familiar or more specialized types of knowledge beyond that given in the text. On average, they have about a 50% probability of performing Level 4 tasks correctly; with Level 5 tasks, their likelihood of responding correctly decreases to 40%.

Similar kinds of interpretations can be made using the information presented for the document and quantitative literacy scales. For example, someone who is at 200 on the quantitative scale has, on average, a 67% chance of responding correctly to Level 1 tasks. His or her likelihood of responding correctly decreases to 45% for Level 2 tasks, 20% for Level 3 tasks, 6% for Level 4 tasks and only 2% for Level 5 tasks. Similarly, readers with a proficiency of 300 on the quantitative scale would have a probability of 95% or higher of responding correctly to tasks in Levels 1 and 2. Their average probability would decrease to 78% for Level 3 tasks, 58% for Level 4 and 20% for Level 5.

Conclusion

One of the goals of large-scale surveys is to provide a set of information that can inform policy makers and help them during the decision-making process. Presenting information in a way that will enhance understanding of what has been measured and what conclusions may be drawn from the data is important to reaching this goal. This chapter has presented a framework for understanding the consistency of task responses demonstrated by adults from a number of countries. This framework identifies a set of variables shown to underlie successful performance on a broad array of literacy tasks. Collectively, these variables provide a means for moving away from interpreting survey results in terms of discrete tasks or a single number and towards identifying levels of performance that have generalizability and validity across assessments and groups.

The knowledge and understanding such a framework provides contribute to the evolving concept of test design as more than merely assigning a numerical value (or position) to an individual based on his or her responses to a set of tasks, but rather, to assigning meaning and interpretability to this number. As concern ceases to centre on discrete behaviours or isolated observations and concentrates more on providing a meaningful score, a higher level of measurement is reached (Messick 1989).

References

Kirsch, Irwin S. and Peter Mosenthal. "Interpreting the IEA Reading/Literacy Scales." In *Methodological Issues in Comparative Educational Studies: The Case of the IEA Reading Literacy Study*. Edited by M. Binkley, K. Rust and M. Winglee. Washington, D.C.: National Center for Education Statistics, U.S. Department of Education, 1993.

Kirsch, Irwin S., et al. *Adult Literacy in America: A First Look at the Results of the National Adult Literacy Survey*. Washington, D.C.: National Center for Education Statistics, U.S. Department of Education, 1993.

Montigny, Gilles, Karen Kelly and Stan Jones. *Adult Literacy in Canada: Results of a National Study*. Ottawa: Minister of Industry, Science and Technology (Statistics Canada, Catalogue no. 89-525E), 1991.

Messick, S. "Validity." In *Educational Measurement*, 3rd ed. Edited by R. Linn. New York: Macmillan, 1989.

Appendix C

International standard occupational classification breakdowns at the major, sub-major and minor group titles

Major group 1: **Legislators, senior officials and managers**

Legislators and senior officials
Legislators
Senior government officials
Traditional chiefs and heads of villages
Senior officials of special-interest organisations
Corporate managers[1]
Directors and chief executives
Production and operations department managers
Other department managers
General managers[2]
General managers

Major group 2: **Professionals**

Physical, mathematical and engineering science professionals
Physicists, chemists and related professionals
Mathematicians, statisticians and related professionals
Computing professionals
Architects, engineers and related professionals
Life science and health professionals
Life science professionals
Health professionals (except nursing)
Nursing and midwifery professionals

---

1. This group is intended to include persons who—as directors, chief executives or department managers—manage enterprises or organisations, or departments, requiring a total of three or more managers.

2. This group is intended to include persons who manage enterprises, or in some cases organisations, on their own behalf, or on behalf of the proprietor, with some non-managerial help and the assistance of no more than one other manager who should also be classified in this sub-major group as, in most cases, the tasks will be broader than those of a specialised manager in a larger enterprise or organisation. Non-managerial staff should be classified according to their specific tasks.

Teaching professionals
>   College, university and higher education teaching professionals
>   Secondary education teaching professionals
>   Primary and pre-primary education teaching professionals
>   Special education teaching professionals
>   Other teaching professionals

Other professionals
>   Business professionals
>   Legal professionals
>   Archivists, librarians and related information professionals
>   Social science and related professionals
>   Writers and creative or performing artists
>   Religious professionals

Major group 3:   Technicians and associate professionals

Physical and engineering science associate professionals
>   Physical and engineering science technicians
>   Computer associate professionals
>   Optical and electronic equipment operators
>   Ship and aircraft controllers and technicians
>   Safety and quality inspectors

Life science and health associate professionals
>   Life science technicians and related associate professionals
>   Modern health associate professionals (except nursing)
>   Nursing and midwifery associate professionals
>   Traditional medicine practitioners and faith healers

Teaching associate professionals
>   Primary education teaching associate professionals
>   Pre-primary education teaching associate professionals
>   Special education teaching associate professionals
>   Other teaching associate professionals

Other associate professionals
>   Finance and sales associate professionals
>   Business services agents and trade brokers
>   Administrative associate professionals
>   Customs, tax and related government associate professionals
>   Police inspectors and detectives
>   Social work associate professionals
>   Artistic, entertainment and sports associate professionals
>   Religious associate professionals

Major group 4:   Clerks

Office clerks
>   Secretaries and keyboard-operating clerks
>   Numerical clerks
>   Material-recording and transport clerks
>   Library, mail and related clerks
>   Other office clerks

Customer services clerks
    Cashiers, tellers and related clerks
    Client information clerks

Major group 5:   Service workers and shop and market sales workers

Personal and protective services workers
    Travel attendants and related workers
    Housekeeping and restaurant services workers
    Personal care and related workers
    Other personal services workers
    Astrologers, fortune-tellers and related workers
    Protective services workers
Models, salespersons and demonstrators
    Fashion and other models
    Shop salespersons and demonstrators
    Stall and market salespersons

Major group 6:   Skilled agricultural and fishery workers

Market-oriented skilled agricultural and fishery workers
    Market gardeners and crop growers
    Market-oriented animal producers and related workers
    Market-oriented crop and animal producers
    Forestry and related workers
    Fishery workers, hunters and trappers
Subsistence agricultural and fishery workers
    Subsistence agricultural and fishery workers

Major group 7:   Craft and related trades workers

Extraction and building trades workers
    Miners, shotfirers, stone cutters and carvers
    Building frame and related trades workers
    Building finishers and related trades workers
    Painters, building structure cleaners and related trades workers
Metal, machinery and related trades workers
    Metal moulders, welders, sheet-metal workers, structural-metal preparers, and related trades workers
    Blacksmiths, tool-makers and related trades workers
    Machinery mechanics and fitters
    Electrical and electronic equipment mechanics and fitters
Precision, handicraft, printing and related trades workers
    Precision workers in metal and related materials
    Potters, glass-makers and related trades workers
    Handicraft workers in wood, textile, leather and related materials
    Printing and related trades workers
Other craft and related trades workers
    Food processing and related trades workers
    Wood treaters, cabinet-makers and related trades workers
    Textile, garment and related trades workers

Pelt, leather and shoemaking trades workers

Major group 8: Plant and machine operators and assemblers

Stationary-plant and related operators
  Mining- and mineral-processing-plant operators
  Metal-processing-plant operators
  Glass, ceramics and related plant operators
  Wood-processing- and papermaking-plant operators
  Chemical-processing-plant operators
  Power-production and related plant operators
  Automated-assembly-line and industrial-robot operators
Machine operators and assemblers
  Metal- and mineral-products machine operators
  Chemical-products machine operators
  Rubber- and plastic-products machine operators
  Wood-products machine operators
  Printing-, binding- and paper-products machine operators
  Textile-, fur- and leather-products machine operators
  Food and related products machine operators
  Assemblers
  Other machine operators and assemblers
Drivers and mobile-plant operators
  Locomotive-engine drivers and related workers
  Motor-vehicle drivers
  Agricultural and other mobile-plant operators
  Ships' deck crews and related workers

Major group 9: Elementary occupations

Sales and services elementary occupations
  Street vendors and related workers
  Shoe cleaning and other street services elementary occupations
  Domestic and related helpers, cleaners and launderers
  Building caretakers, window and related cleaners
  Messengers, porters, doorkeepers and related workers
  Garbage collectors and related labourers
Agricultural, fishery and related labourers
  Agricultural, fishery and related labourers
Labourers in mining, construction, manufacturing and transport
  Mining and construction labourers
  Manufacturing labourers
  Transport labourers and freight handlers

Major group 0: Armed forces

Armed forces
  Armed forces

Statistics Canada – Catalogue no. 89-551-XPE